Social Media

Peggy J. Parks

San Diego, CA

About the Author

Peggy J. Parks holds a bachelor of science degree from Aquinas College in Grand Rapids, Michigan, where she graduated magna cum laude. An author who has written dozens of educational books on a wide variety of topics for young people, Parks lives in Muskegon, Michigan, a town she says inspires her writing because of its location on the shores of beautiful Lake Michigan.

© 2017 ReferencePoint Press, Inc.
Printed in the United States

For more information, contact:
ReferencePoint Press, Inc.
PO Box 27779
San Diego, CA 92198
www. ReferencePointPress.com

LIBRARY OF CONGRESS CATALOGING-IN-PUBLICATION DATA

Names: Parks, Peggy J., 1951- author.
Title: Social media / by Peggy J. Parks.
Description: San Diego, CA : ReferencePoint Press, Inc., 2017. | Series:
   Digital issues | Includes bibliographical references and index.
Identifiers: LCCN 2016018761 (print) | LCCN 2016022801 (ebook) | ISBN
   9781601529923 (hardback) | ISBN 9781601529930 (eBook)
Subjects: LCSH: Online social networks--Juvenile literature. | Social
   media--Juvenile literature.
Classification: LCC HM742 .P3723 2017 (print) | LCC HM742 (ebook) | DDC
   302.30285--dc23
LC record available at https://lccn.loc.gov/2016018761

CONTENTS

A Global Community

In late January 2004 a Harvard University sophomore named Mark Zuckerberg decided to create a new website. A computer programming whiz and talented game creator, Zuckerberg thought his fellow students would benefit from a new kind of site: one that served as an online directory with photos and profiles, as well as a social networking tool that helped people find each other and stay in touch with friends. He worked on the site night and day and finished it in just a week. On February 4, 2004, Zuckerberg launched what he called Thefacebook—and people were immediately captivated by it. Within two weeks of its launch, forty-eight hundred students, alumni, and faculty members had registered, and the number continued to climb. "I have no idea why it's so popular," Zuckerberg said during an interview with the campus magazine *Harvard Crimson*. "I was pretty surprised."[1] He had no way of knowing how much and how fast his creation's popularity would soar.

Explosive Growth

By 2005 more than 5 million users at colleges and universities throughout the United States were registered users of Thefacebook. Zuckerberg soon shortened its name to Facebook, and the following year he released the site to the public. From that point on, membership grew exponentially. In 2009 there were 360 million users; the number jumped to 608 million the following year—and by 2013 membership topped 1 billion. Today, according to the social media marketing research firm Smart Insights, Facebook has more active users worldwide than any other social media platform. YouTube holds second place, followed by Twitter, Google+, Instagram, LinkedIn, Pinterest, Tumblr, Badoo, and Myspace (in that order).

The popularity of social media differs based on age. For example, Facebook was initially designed for college students but is now most popular among middle-aged adults. Millions of teens and young adults still use Facebook, but they tend to favor other social media such as Snapchat, Kik, Wechat, Tumblr, and Instagram. Although young people have their own reasons for *unliking* Facebook, research has shown that many leave because it has become so popular with older adults. Parents who originally joined to keep an eye on what their kids were doing, for instance, may have found they enjoyed Facebook and decided to stick around. This likely affected the site's appeal for younger users, as Nico Lang writes in the *Washington Post*: "It's hard to look cool when you're hanging out with Mom and Dad."[2]

All in all, more than 2 billion people worldwide are active on social media—a full 30 percent of the global population. One factor in its burgeoning popularity is the growth of smartphone ownership. According to the Pew Research Center, nearly 90 percent of American adults aged eighteen to forty-nine and more than 70 percent of teens have a smartphone. "The growing ubiquity of cell phones, especially the rise of smartphones, has made social networking just a finger tap away,"[3] the group writes. Today social media has become such an integral part of people's lives that they often find it difficult to imagine a time when it did not exist.

> "Beyond making new friends, social media is a major way that teens interact with their existing friends."[4]
>
> —Amanda Lenhart, a senior research specialist at the Pew Research Center.

How People Use Social Media

When asked why they like social media, people offer a variety of reasons. By far the most common is friendship; they go online to stay in touch with friends and make new ones. A 2015 study by

More than 2 billion people—or 30 percent of the world's population—are active on social media. A primary reason for this is the global adoption of smartphones.

GlobalWebIndex found that staying in touch with friends is the number one reason why people use social media. This is true of all ages, including teens, as the Pew Research Center's Amanda Lenhart explains: "Social media plays a critical role in connecting teens to new friends, allowing teens to learn more about new friends and get to know them better. . . . Beyond making new friends, social media is a major way that teens interact with their existing friends."[4]

Also, according to the GlobalWebIndex study, a leading reason why people use social media is to keep track of the latest news and current events. This is especially true of Twitter and Facebook, both of which are popular for breaking news. The tendency of people to get their news from social media is highest among smartphone users. According to the American Press Institute, people who own smartphones are two and half times as likely to get news through social media as those without the devices.

People have other reasons for being fans of social media, such as enjoying funny and/or entertaining content, sharing their photos and videos, and being able to get into conversations and express their opinions. But along with the enjoyment, there are also negative aspects to social media. One downside is anonymity; as with the Internet in general, many social media platforms allow people to sign up without revealing their true names, which enables those who bully, harass, or abuse others to do so without anyone knowing who they are. "This is the kind of behavior that makes the whole Internet, and particularly social media, less productive and enjoyable for all," says Tommy Landry, a social media consultant from Austin, Texas. "Being offensive anonymously is not only cowardly, it shows a lack of character. We should all be better than that." Beyond anonymity (and associated bad behaviors), people may have other negative online experiences that cause them to reject social media or take a break from it for a while. "As with any communication medium," says Landry, "it comes with its ups and downs, pros and cons."[5] Overall, however, Landry and many others believe social media makes the world a decidedly better place, whereas others want nothing to do with it. Whether Internet users love social media or hate it, there is every reason to believe it is here to stay.

> "Being offensive anonymously is not only cowardly, it shows a lack of character. We should all be better than that."[5]
>
> —Tommy Landry, a social media consultant from Austin, Texas.

CHAPTER ONE

Human Interaction and Relationships

Emily Rose Radecki, a college student from Indiana, loves to spend time with her best friend, Kate. They talk about everything and lean on each other when either of them is feeling down. The girls have a great deal in common; both love music and singing, enjoy watching many of the same TV shows, and have similar taste in clothing and foods. "Deep down I think it's the little things like this that keep us so tightly bonded with one another," says Emily. "Because we are interested in the same things, we quite possibly have similar ideas about life itself." Their religious faith is another bond between them, an "important thread that keeps us so tightly woven."[6]

For the most part, Emily and Kate's friendship is much like friendships between other girls their age. There is one important difference, however—they have never met in person. In 2012 they "met" on Facebook through a mutual friend and hit it off right away. Soon they were chatting online and texting, and that led to virtual get-togethers on FaceTime. "Whenever we meet on FaceTime," says Emily, "it's like I'm joking with any of my friends I've actually met. We can be super weird and make one another laugh or talk about real emotions."[7] Until she became so close to Kate, Emily was skeptical about friendships that revolved around social media. She has changed her mind about that but still thinks relationships like the one she has with Kate are rare.

Digital Friendships

Emily may be right about the depth of her relationship with Kate, but research has shown that young people who meet online often develop friendships. This was one finding of a 2015 survey by the Pew Research Center that involved 1,060 teens. The survey, which was designed to gather information about young people's Internet activity, found that 57 percent of teens have met at least one new friend online, and 29 percent have met at least five. "For American teens, making friends isn't just confined to the school yard, playing field or neighborhood," says Pew's associate director of research Amanda Lenhart, who led the project. According to Lenhart, the relationship between these online friends is usually limited to their online activities, since only about 20 percent of teens have met an online friend in person. "Most of these friendships stay in the digital space,"[8] she says.

The Pew survey also revealed that teen friendships are strengthened and challenged within social media environments. "Social media helps teens feel more connected to their friends' feelings and daily lives," says Lenhart, "and also offers teens a place to receive support from others during challenging times."[9] More than 80 percent of the teens surveyed said that social media makes them feel more connected to information about their friends' lives, and 70 percent said they feel better connected to their friends' feelings through social media.

Although parents have a tendency to worry when their teenagers meet new friends online, experts are not too concerned by the trend. They emphasize that online friendships are fine as long as teens realize the limitations of such relationships and take measures to keep themselves safe, which should be standard practice anytime they use the Internet. According to Georgetown University psychology professor Andrea Bonior, making friends online is "kind of a new reality." She adds, "We're getting to the point where, for the upcoming generation, this is just the way it is."[10]

> "Social media helps teens feel more connected to their friends' feelings and daily lives, and also offers teens a place to receive support from others during challenging times."[9]
>
> —Amanda Lenhart, associate director of research at the Pew Research Center.

Teens Meeting Teens

Both teenage girls and boys make friends online, but the Pew survey showed some differences based on gender. Boys, for instance, make friends online more often than girls do. Also, they meet people in different ways. Girls most often make friends on social media, such as Facebook and Instagram. Boys meet friends on social media, too, but are more likely to make friends while playing online video games. Lenhart says that many teen gamers, especially boys, connect with their fellow players using voice connections, which allows them to engage in "collaboration, conversation and trash-talking."[11]

Technology and Internet safety advocate Larry Magid says it is not surprising that online gaming is how boys most often make friends. "Many of today's online games involve interacting, competing or cooperating with other players," he says. One of the most obvious benefits of online gaming is the ability for teens to

Video chat apps such as Facetime and Skype allow people to have virtual get-togethers. In some cases, people have developed close relationships through these and other social media platforms without ever having met in person.

meet and socialize with other young people. But, Magid adds, "it can also be a learning venue for a variety of useful skills including, of course, collaboration and planning." He personally observed someone who had learned a lot from online gaming. "When I was in Turkey a few years ago I met a young man with excellent English," recalls Magid. "When I asked him how he learned it, he said it was through chatting during online games."[12]

University of California–Berkeley student DeVante Ellis Brown has met many friends through online gaming. After watching people play *Call of Duty* on the live-streaming gaming platform Twitch, Brown finally joined in and later became a moderator. He views the friends he has made online much as those he knows in real life. "We talk about the same type of things," he says. "Only real difference is I don't see their faces." Brown says that once when he was at a summer camp, he overheard two younger children talking about how they would not see each other for a whole year. The next best thing, they decided, would be to meet online each day to play *Minecraft*. This made an impression on Brown, as he explains: "It really hit me. The way that friendships can form through gaming is so interesting, and we never know what can emerge from it."[13]

Face Time Versus Online

The connection teens have with their online friends is something adults experience as well. Facebook, for instance, brings people together who have lost touch for years and may never have reconnected if not for social media. "Social ties that we once would have abandoned as we left high school, changed jobs and moved from one neighborhood to another now persist online," says Keith N. Hampton, a professor of communication and public policy at Rutgers University. "Today, high-school friends stay with us on Facebook in a way that they wouldn't have done in the past."[14] Hampton says the same is true for professional acquaintances, distant relatives, and others from the various phases of people's lives.

In research with his students, Hampton has found that Internet and smartphone users (especially those who use social media) tend to have a larger number of close friends and more diverse relationships than those who do not make friends online. Technology, according to Hampton, is transforming how people relate to others, and for the most part the results of this are positive. "In our closest relationships," he says, "today's technologies don't replace in-person interaction, they supplement it."[15]

Another communications professional who believes technology can enhance personal relationships is Alice Marwick, an assistant professor of communication and media studies at Fordham University. Marwick cautions against categorizing friendships as real or unreal based solely on whether they are in-person or online. She emphasizes that Internet friendships can definitely be real friendships, and in many cases they involve both online and offline contact. "Most of us fluidly move between on- and off-line social contexts," she says, "and so do our friendships."[16]

> "In our closest relationships, today's technologies don't replace in-person interaction, they supplement it."[15]
>
> —Keith N. Hampton, a professor of communication and public policy at Rutgers University.

In the early 2000s, when Marwick lived in Seattle, Washington, she was part of the LiveJournal blogging community and followed hundreds of people. She remains friends with some of them and keeps in touch regularly through social media. "I've known many of them for close to a decade," says Marwick. "We've written about marriages, miscarriages, Ph.D. programs, moves, breakups, highs and lows. I feel genuine closeness and intimacy with them based on their words, though they are written by people I've never met."[17]

The Essential Human Connection

As beneficial as social media can be for cultivating friendships and making new friends, psychologists widely agree that it cannot—and should not—replace real-life, face-to-face relationships. People may communicate with each other online, have satisfying conversations, and feel close to each other. But according to research psychologist Larry Rosen, this is not the same as humans connecting with each other on a deeper level. He writes: "While we may have hundreds

Unplugged, Reconnected

MIT psychology professor Sherry Turkle has spent three decades studying how online connectivity affects human interaction. One of her most troubling observations is that because of technology (especially smartphones), children seem to lack empathy and the ability to fully understand each other. But Turkle has also seen that the damage can be undone. She cites a 2014 study of sixth graders who attended a device-free summer camp, one where phones, tablet computers, and other electronic gadgets were not allowed. After five technology-free days, the difference in the children was remarkable.

The campers were shown silent videos and an assortment of still photos. They were able to read emotions on people's faces nearly twice as often as a group of children who had just arrived at the camp. What fostered these new empathic responses, according to Turkle, was that camp gave these children the opportunity to actually talk to each other, rather than just interacting via social media. "In conversation, things go best if you pay close attention and learn how to put yourself in someone else's shoes," she says. "This is easier to do without your phone in hand. Conversation is the most human and humanizing thing we can do."

Sherry Turkle, "Stop Googling. Let's Talk," *New York Times*, September 26, 2015. www.nytimes.com.

of Facebook friends—people we never would have met otherwise, with whom we can share many new things—do they really provide the kind of human interaction that is so essential to our emotional health?"[18]

Kate Roberts, a psychologist from Boston, Massachusetts, agrees that essential human contact is missing when people rely so much on online communication. She warns that those who rely heavily on technology for communication are depriving themselves and their loved ones of something precious and invaluable. "When people aren't using face-to-face contact for personal issues, it

A group of friends socializes at a dinner party. Many psychologists argue that while social media is beneficial in many ways it cannot and should not replace real-life, face-to-face relationships.

doesn't fill the intimacy need," says Roberts. "For all the strong reaction out there about Twitter and Facebook allowing emotional expression, it's not necessarily effective. You're not necessarily getting to a resolution like you would (with another person)."[19] Roberts worries that because technology makes communication so easy, people rely on it without considering how they might be losing meaningful connections with people they care about.

Research has shown that people often turn to social media for friendships because online relationships are easier and less complicated than real-life relationships. Massachusetts Institute of Technology (MIT) psychology professor Sherry Turkle refers to this as the "Goldilocks effect." "You can have your friendships at the temperature you want them—not too close, not too distant, just right," she says. Face-to-face relationships require a greater emotional investment because they cultivate empathy—the natural, human reaction to witnessing someone's feelings. "You are able to experience the whole person, the tone of their voice, the way they hold their body, the way they respond to you," says Turkle. "It demands vulnerability—there is no 'just right' distance available when someone makes demands right now."[20]

Nonverbal Communication

One crucial aspect of communication that is missing from online interactions is the presence of nonverbal cues. According to communication and leadership expert Susan Tardanico, only 7 percent of communication is based on what is spoken or written. "A whopping 93% is based on nonverbal body language,"[21] she says. Nonverbal cues include tone of voice, gestures, facial expressions, and the look in someone's eyes, among others.

The online world's lack of nonverbal cues can help people present themselves as they want others to see them. When they post on Facebook or Tumblr, tweet a message, text a friend, or send an e-mail, Tardanico says they can create "an illusion of their choosing." She adds: "They can be whoever they want to be. And without the ability to receive nonverbal cues, their audiences are none the wiser."[22]

> "When people aren't using face-to-face contact for personal issues, it doesn't fill the intimacy need."[19]
>
> —Kate Roberts, a psychologist from Boston, Massachusetts.

When texting or posting to social media, one of the ways people have learned to compensate for the lack of nonverbal elements is to use emoticons and emojis. Originally invented to convey humor or sarcasm in e-mails, emoticons can express everything from sadness and anger to surprise, horror, hilarity, and disrespect. "Voice inflection, body language, facial expression and the pheromones (released during face-to-face interaction): These are all fundamental to establishing human relationships," says Jim Taylor, a psychologist from San Francisco, California. "And they're all missing with most forms of modern technology." Although emoticons cannot replace human emotions, says Taylor, "they're an attempt to add what's missing."[23]

Yet even though emoticons can enrich certain online communications, they fall short of conveying the complex feelings that face-to-face interactions would. This was exemplified during a 2011 text exchange between Sharon Seline and her daughter, who was away at college. Seline asked how things were going, and her daughter answered that everything was fine. She punctuated this assurance with emoticons of smiley faces, bigger smiley faces, and hearts. When their conversation ended, Seline felt assured that everything was going well for her daughter at school. She had no way of knowing that the girl was severely depressed and had been holed up in her dorm room crying—and then attempted suicide that night. "Indeed," says Tardanico, "it's only when we can hear a tone of voice or look into someone's eyes that we're able to know when 'I'm fine' doesn't mean they're fine at all."[24]

Signing In and Tuning Out

Whether social media improves human relationships or interferes with them is often a matter of interpretation and personal opinion. One fact that cannot be denied, however, is how much easier smartphones make it for people to stay in contact with their social networks. Rosen has studied the impact of technology on adults, teens, and children for thirty years, and he is convinced that becoming more digitally connected has made people *less* sociable. According to Rosen, smartphones, along with computers and the growth of social media, have been "game changers" in human interaction, and not in a good way. "The total effect," says Rosen, "has been to allow us to connect more with the people in our virtual world—but communicate less with those who are in our real world."[25]

Rosen acknowledges that there is a connection between people's real and virtual worlds, since many of their online friends are also friends in real life. But he emphasizes that the more time they spend online with their Internet friends, the less time they have to communicate and connect on a deeper level with people in the real world. "With smartphone in hand, we face a constant barrage of alerts, notifications, vibrations and beeps," says Rosen, "warning us that something seemingly important has happened and we must pay attention. . . . If we are constantly checking in with our virtual worlds, this leaves little time for our real-world relationships."[26]

In a September 2015 article titled "Stop Googling. Let's Talk," Turkle discussed research she has done with MIT students about what happens to face-to-face conversation "in a world where so many people say they would rather text than talk." Turkle's students have described how it is now normal to carry on a real-life conversation while simultaneously being aware of one's phone.

A young woman is preoccupied with her smartphone while sitting with friends. Some believe that the barrage of alerts, notifications, vibrations, and beeps of smartphones are a constant distraction to their owners from real world communication and relationships.

Facebook as a Relationship Booster

Social media users who want to announce that they are a couple can do so in various ways, from choosing the "in a relationship" status to posting photos and videos of themselves being affectionate. In 2015 Catalina Toma, a communication science professor at the University of Wisconsin–Madison, conducted a study to explore the link between people's Facebook presence and romantic relationships. Toma had college-age dating couples fill out questionnaires that measured their feelings about the relationship and how committed they felt to their partners. She also monitored their Facebook activity and noted how they presented themselves. Six months later she followed up with all couples to see if they were still together.

Toma found that certain Facebook activities enhanced people's feelings of commitment and also played a role in whether they stayed with their partners. For instance, people who used the status "in a relationship," posted photos with their partner, and wrote on their partner's wall were more likely to stay together than those who did not. Toma says it is well known that the claims people make about themselves in public likely reflect their perceptions of themselves. "Now," she says, "we're finding that these public self-presentations performed on Facebook also affect how people feel about a relationship partner." As for why public displays of relationship status can influence a couple's longevity, Toma compares it with weddings. "People declare their love, they make vows in front of friends and family, they take photographs, and they exchange rings," she says. "Online claims are very meaningful psychologically, and I think a big reason for that is the access to this diverse and wide audience."

Quoted in Jenny Price, "The Couple Who Facebooks Together, Stays Together," news release, University of Wisconsin–Madison, July 24, 2015. http://news.wisc.edu.

The students were matter-of-fact about this but also, she says, "described a sense of loss." According to Turkle, studies of conversation have shown that when two people are talking face-to-face, if a cell phone is visible (either between them or within their peripheral vision), it changes the content of their conversation and whether they feel a sense of connection. "People keep the conversation on topics where they won't mind being interrupted," she says. "They don't feel as invested in each other. Even a silent phone disconnects us."[27]

Seeking a Balance

People disagree about how social media has affected human interaction and relationships. Because friendships often develop through online connections, many view this as a natural extension of real-life networks; just another way of making friends. But many experts warn that people need the human element, the emotional aspect, the intimacy—qualities that are only possible through face-to-face contact. Because the popularity of Tumblr, Twitter, Facebook, Instagram, and other such online platforms is not likely to decline, achieving a balance between online and offline relationships would be a beneficial goal for anyone who participates in social media.

CHAPTER TWO

Sharing and Oversharing

In March 2015, when her husband, Alex, died suddenly from a massive brain aneurysm, Kristina Doan Gruenberg was devastated. They had been together for ten years, and she could not imagine a future without him. Her family and friends showered her with love and support, but Gruenberg often preferred to be alone. Facebook, she says, became her "lifeline to the outside world—one that I could turn on or off at any time depending on my roller coaster of emotions."[28] As her friends posted memories and photos of her husband, she found comfort in being by herself and scrolling through them.

After Alex's memorial service, Gruenberg wrote a tribute to him and posted it on Facebook. The supportive response she received was overwhelming. People she had not heard from in years, some of whom had experienced tragic losses of their own, sent her private messages and posted on her page. This was immensely helpful to her. "I went from feeling like no one could possibly understand what I was going through as a young widow, to realizing that I knew people who were going through the same thing."[29]

Reaching Out

After someone has experienced a loss or endured some kind of personal trauma, it can be therapeutic to talk about it. In this way social media serves as virtual group therapy, in which someone reveals painful circumstances or losses and his or her friends and/or followers reach out to offer comfort, support, and hope. "Social media can act as a social buffer or catalyst for people's pain and loneliness," says Tomas Chamorro-Premuzic, a professor of business psychology at University College London. "It is a cry for warmth and sympathy in an otherwise superficial and narcissistic environment."[30]

Another psychology professional who believes social media can benefit people as they work through emotional pain is Garry Hare, director of the School of Psychology at Fielding Graduate University in Santa Barbara, California. For the person who is grieving, he says, social media becomes a "community that comes together and says you are not alone. And that helps." According to Hare, the collective support and comfort can be very beneficial. In fact, it can help not only the person who is grieving but also those who want to reach out but have hesitated to do so. "In the old days," says Hare, "you had to go knock on your neighbor's door when something was wrong. But not very many of us did it because we didn't know what to say. We were just not equipped. You could send them soup. You can send them a note. Now, the distance provided by social media is extraordinarily safer and that doesn't make it less meaningful."[31]

Young people often turn to social media when they are troubled, such as when a beloved celebrity dies. In early October 2015 thirteen-year-old Caleb Logan Bratayley died suddenly from what was later found to be an undiagnosed heart condition. The teen, one of the stars of a reality TV–style YouTube series called *Bratayley*, was extremely popular among preteens and teens, and his death hit them hard. When his mother posted the tragic news on Instagram, thousands of his young fans responded there, as well as on Vine, YouTube, and Twitter. Using the hashtag #ripcaleb, they mourned his death and celebrated his life, while offering prayers and healing to his family. One of his young fans tweeted: "You died

> "Social media can act as a social buffer or catalyst for people's pain and loneliness."[30]
>
> —Tomas Chamorro-Premuzic, a professor of business psychology at University College London.

Young people often turn to social media when they are troubled, such as when a beloved celebrity dies. Publicists, family, and friends of a deceased celebrity often use social media to announce the tragedy to fans and give them an opportunity to share feelings and tributes.

[too] young Caleb Logan. Heaven gained another angel."[32] Others talked about how they would personally mourn Caleb, such as holding candlelight vigils in their hometowns.

Bereavement experts say this collective outpouring of sadness and support can be healthy for young people. Even though they may not have known Caleb personally, they feel like they did, which means they mourn his death—and it hurts. According to Andy McNiel, chief executive officer of the National Alliance for Grieving Children, when kids turn to each other and offer support on social media, it can help with the healing process. "It's the established way they connect and interact with each other," says McNiel. "Kids feel very comfortable dealing with each other at times like this."[33]

Sharing, Sharing, and More Sharing

Along with giving and receiving support during hard times, people also use social media to post and tweet about happy, memorable occasions. How much and how often people share depends on their personal preference. Some users limit their posting and tweeting to photos, humorous memes, and inspirational messages. Others share the most minute details of their lives, from describing what they eat for each meal to checking in whenever they travel to a new location.

This penchant for sharing what many people view as far too much information is commonly referred to as oversharing, and it is a subject of interest among researchers. "Why do people overshare?" asks psychologist Jennifer Golbeck. "It's not because they don't know how to keep their thoughts private; they choose not to." One widely accepted theory for why people overshare is known as the online disinhibition effect. "The concept is simple," says Golbeck. "People lose inhibitions online that they would have in person."[34] Factors that play a role in this include anonymity, the feeling one is invisible while online, missing nonverbal cues from other people, and a sense that the online world is not real.

Researcher Bodo Lang, a senior lecturer at New Zealand's University of Auckland, says that people who overshare on social media are often lulled into a false sense of security. They forget that their audience is potentially much bigger than a group of friends; their words could be read by people all over the world. "Social media [gives people] a stage," says Lang. On it, he explains, people perform without fear, but also without any of the cues they would normally get when speaking to an audience in real life—cues that could prevent them from sharing more than they should. "Removal of social cues is a really big issue," he says. "You don't get them until it's too late."[35] Lang theorizes that most oversharing is unintentional; a product of people's inability to monitor their own behavior and think through potential consequences before posting.

Even though social media is wildly popular with young people, even they have concerns about oversharing. During the 2015 Pew Research survey, for instance, 88 percent of teens said they believe people share too much information about themselves on social media. Moreover, much of this information negatively affected teens who saw it. For example, when asked if they had seen posts about events to which they were not invited, 53 percent said yes. More than 40 percent had seen someone post things on social media about them that they could not change or control, and 21 percent reported feeling worse about their own lives because of what others posted. "Even as social media connects teens to friends' feelings and experiences," says Amanda Lenhart, "the sharing that occurs on these platforms can have negative consequences. Sharing can veer into oversharing."[36]

Lost College Dreams

In many cases oversharing leads to embarrassment or the need to apologize for insensitive remarks, but usually nothing more serious than that. Depending on the individual situation, however, those who unwisely overshare can seriously damage their reputations or future plans. "People just can't stop posting things they shouldn't," says McAfee online security expert Robert Siciliano, "which often have long-term negative effects on their personal and professional lives."[37]

> "People just can't stop posting things they shouldn't, which often have long-term negative effects on their personal and professional lives."[37]
>
> —Robert Siciliano, an online security expert with McAfee.

High school students who use social media may not realize that posting the wrong thing could hurt their chances of being accepted into college. In a July and August 2015 survey of nearly four hundred college admissions officers, Kaplan Test Prep found that 40 percent of participants visited applicants' social media pages to learn more about the students. The officers had various reasons for perusing the teens' social media activity, from verifying awards they claim to have received to following up on anonymous tips about inappropriate behavior. "The growth of social media hasn't made [the] college admissions process a whole new ballgame, but it's definitely changed the rules," says Yariv Alpher, Kaplan's executive director of research. "What you post online can and may be used in your favor or against you, so it's important to think about what

A young woman anxiously looks through the mail for college acceptance letters. Professionals warn teenagers to be careful about how they use social media as many college admissions officers will research applicants' online behavior. Their findings can impact an acceptance decision.

you share. When in doubt, the best strategy may be to keep it to yourself."[38]

One high school senior's offensive Twitter remarks prevented her from being accepted by an elite East Coast college. In 2012 the girl was attending a campus information session at Bowdoin College in Brunswick, Maine. During the presentation she looked around at her fellow attendees and fired off one insulting, profanity-laced tweet after another about them. "It was incredibly unusual and foolish of her to do that," says Scott A. Meiklejohn, Bowdoin's dean of admissions and financial aid. As it turned out, the student's grades were not competitive enough for her to be accepted at the school. But even if she were a top student, her online behavior would have sabotaged her admission chances, as Meiklejohn explains: "We would have wondered about the judgment of someone who spends their time on their mobile phone and makes such awful remarks."[39]

Think First, Tweet Later

Because social media is used by humans, and all humans make mistakes, it is not unusual for people to post or tweet things they later end up regretting. This was revealed in a July 2015 survey by the market research firm YouGov, in which 57 percent of social media users said they have posted or texted something they later regretted. When asked about their biggest regret, most respondents said it was not properly considering their remarks before posting or tweeting them, and in the process sounding foolish. Other regrets included comments made in the heat of the moment that offended a friend or comments that offended many people.

One interesting finding of the study was the time frame of these regrettable remarks. The researchers found that it usually happened late at night, when the individuals were at home, tired, and/or drinking alcohol. "There are three rules people need to live by," says Don S. Dizon, an associate professor at Harvard Medical School who lectures on safety and social media. "Don't tweet or post when fatigued, inebriated, or angry. Most bad behavior is related to one of those three."

Quoted in Alyssa Giacobbe, "6 Ways Social Media Can Ruin Your Life," *Boston Globe Magazine*, May 21, 2014. www.bostonglobe.com.

Job Hunters Beware

Unwise sharing on social media can also result in lost career opportunities. According to the talent network CareerBuilder, more than half of companies now review job applicants' social media activity before making final hiring decisions. "Every recruiter that I know, every [human resources] person that I know are all using tools that integrate social media into the way that companies filter through applicants for jobs,"[40] says Mary Ellen Slayter, a career expert with online job search company, Monster.

One important reason for reviewing social media activity before hiring someone is to find out whether the person would be a good representative of the company's image. For example, applicants who dress impeccably and act poised and professional during an interview may hurt their chances of being hired if social media show them talking or acting in unbecoming ways. "Part of what companies do when they [search] for you on social media is to see how you conduct yourself," says Marcie Kirk Holland, a project manager at the University of California–Davis Internship and Career Center. "They want to know how you'll interact with your co-workers and more importantly their customers or potential customers."[41]

Derogatory social media posts or tweets can also come back to haunt people who already have jobs. According to CareerBuilder, 28 percent of employers have reportedly fired people for using the Internet for non-work-related activities (such as posting or tweeting while they were supposed to be working) during the workday, and 18 percent have fired employees because of something they posted on social media. "Social media is booming with networking opportunities and the chance to share your accomplishments," said Rosemary Haefner, CareerBuilder's chief human resources officer. "But it could also lead to the end of your career if used incorrectly."[42]

> "What you post online can and may be used in your favor or against you, so it's important to think about what you share."[38]
>
> —Yariv Alpher, executive director of research for Kaplan Test Prep.

In 2015 Kaitlyn Walls was fired even before she started her new job. The twenty-seven-year-old woman from The Colony, Texas (a suburb of Dallas), was hired for a job at a day care center. She was happy to finally have steady work so she could pay her bills and support her daughter—but on social media, she revealed her inner negativity. "I start my new job today," Walls posted on her Facebook page. "But I absolutely hate working at day care. I just really hate being around a lot of kids." The post sparked outrage, and people immediately started criticizing Walls. When the day care center operators found out what she had written, they told her not to bother coming to work. "It really was a big mistake," she says, adding that the situation taught her a tough lesson. "I'm not going to post anything like it ever no matter how I feel."[43]

Sharing strong or undiplomatic opinions on social media can have unintended consequences. Once a message is posted it can race through social media. A person can be shamed forever by one bad decision.

Reckless Revelations

It is common for people who enjoy sharing on social media to tell friends and followers when something exciting happens. For instance, those who are going on vacation often post about their upcoming plans and continue to post while they are away. Although people may enjoy these posts and the accompanying photos, vacationers could be making a major mistake. "Posting vacation plans on social media is like inviting thieves to your home," says the security company Sonitrol Pacific. The group emphasizes that people should never publicize their vacation plans or post pictures until after they return home. "Posting information about your travel plans can increase the risk of burglaries or break-ins as criminals are now targeting social media to find victims, even if your account is private."[44]

In December 2014 a woman from Surfside Beach, South Carolina, posted on Facebook about her upcoming weeklong vacation in Nassau, Bahamas. While she was gone she shared many pictures of the beautiful sandy beaches and lovely island scenery. Unfortunately, she returned home to find that burglars had broken in and stole numerous valuables. Police who investigated discovered that the woman had been specifically targeted because of what she posted on Facebook, and the thieves were Facebook friends.

Ruined Lives

One of the biggest downfalls of sharing strong opinions on social media is that once something has been posted, it is out of the person's control. Even if he or she has a change of heart and deletes or cancels the post, one or more individuals may have already seen it and passed it on to others. From there the message or photo can race through social media like wildfire, leaving catastrophe in its wake. This is social media at its ugliest; what happens when someone makes a bad decision and is repeatedly, relentlessly shamed for it by an angry, vengeful mob. "There's a real cruelty that comes with this mob mentality," says Father James Martin, a Roman Catholic priest and editor at large of *America* magazine. "I sometimes compare it to bullies in a schoolyard all ganging up on [a] person who, for one second, said the wrong thing."[45]

This is what happened to Justine Sacco in December 2013—and it nearly ruined her life. At the time, Sacco was a public relations executive at a firm in New York City. She was on her way to Cape Town, South Africa, to visit family. While on layover at London's Heathrow Airport, Sacco dashed off a tweet that said: "Going to Africa. Hope I don't get AIDS. Just kidding. I'm white!"[46] Later, Sacco would explain the point of her tweet: to

> "There's a real cruelty that comes with this [online] mob mentality. I sometimes compare it to bullies in a schoolyard all ganging up on [a] person who, for one second, said the wrong thing."[45]
>
> —Father James Martin, a Roman Catholic priest and editor at large of *America* magazine.

"Oversharenting"

It is a common practice for parents to post about their children, whether to show milestones in a baby's life or chronicle a teen's artistic or sports accomplishments. "Sharing the joys and challenges of parenthood and documenting children's lives publicly has become a social norm," says Sarah J. Clark, a research scientist in the University of Michigan's Department of Pediatrics. Oversharing (or oversharenting) can lead to problems, however. "Parents may share information that their child finds embarrassing or too personal when they're older but once it's out there, it's hard to undo," says Clark.

In a March 2015 poll by the University of Michigan CS Mott Children's Hospital, 74 percent of respondents said they know a parent who has shared too much about a child on social media. This included embarrassing stories, information that could identify a child's location, or photos that could be perceived as inappropriate. Security experts warn that one of the risks of oversharenting is that strangers can steal children's photos and reshare them as if the children were their own—which has innumerable security implications. Also, children's photos can make them the target of cruel jokes and cyberbullying. "Parents are responsible for their child's privacy and need to be thoughtful about how much they share on social media," says Clark, "so they can enjoy the benefits of camaraderie but also protect their children's privacy today and in the future."

Quoted in University of Michigan CS Mott Children's Hospital, "'Sharenting' Trends: Do Parents Share Too Much About Their Kids on Social Media?," March 16, 2015. www.mott children.org.

mock the ignorance of many white people who view AIDS as an African illness. "To me it was so insane of a comment for anyone to make," says Sacco. "I thought there was no way that anyone could possibly think it was literal."[47] She was wrong, however. People interpreted her post precisely opposite of what she intended—and then took it upon themselves to destroy her.

Sacco had fewer than two hundred Twitter followers, but someone forwarded the tweet to Gawker Media editor Sam Biddle—who had fifteen thousand followers. Furious over what he viewed as a hateful, racist remark, Biddle retweeted it, and the abuse began immediately. Sacco was bombarded by tens of thousands of angry tweets, many of which were accusatory, profane, and threatening. Her "Twitter feed had become a horror show," says Jon Ronson, author of the book *So You've Been Publicly Shamed*. He says people's collective outrage over the tweet "had become not just an ideological crusade against her perceived bigotry but also a form of idle entertainment." Not only was Sacco crucified by Twitter users, she was also ridiculed in numerous media stories and subsequently fired from her job. As Ronson explains, that "one stupid tweet blew up Justine Sacco's life."[48]

What happened to Sacco illustrates the ugly side of sharing on social media: people piling on, one after another, to shame and punish someone who has angered them. But there are also innumerable positive aspects, such as people sharing their joys with one other or reaching out to support someone who is in pain. Whether sharing on social media is a force for good or bad is largely a matter of personal opinion.

CHAPTER THREE

Social Media and Mental Health

As enjoyable, informative, and entertaining as social media can be, it also affects people in negative ways. This is especially true of adolescents; because of their age and all the changes occurring in their bodies, they may sometimes feel uncertain and insecure. When experiencing such feelings, perusing other teens' social media pages, posts, and tweets can fuel young people's insecurity and make them feel worse. "Look," says sixteen-year-old Sasha, as she slowly scrolls through her Instagram feed. "See: pretty coffee, pretty girl, cute cat, beach trip. It's all like that. Everyone looks like they're having the best day ever, all the time." Sometimes this really gets to Sasha; looking at friends' feeds, she says, "makes you feel like everyone has it together but you."[49] Sasha is aware that her mind is playing tricks on her at times like that; her friends are probably no more "together" than she is. Still, those moments of uncertainty and inferiority can be really tough for kids to cope with.

Adolescent psychologists say that perceptions like Sasha's are common. According to Jill Emanuele, a clinical psychologist with the Child Mind Institute, what young people see on social media can reinforce self-image problems and self-doubt. "Kids view social media through the lens of their own lives," she says. "If they're struggling to stay on top of things or suffering from low self-esteem, they're more likely to interpret images of peers having fun as confirmation that they're doing badly compared to their friends."[50]

This can be distressful for young people and can even lead to psychological disorders such as depression.

Potential Risks of Heavy Use

Since few studies have focused on the association between social media and adolescent mental health, whether such an association exists is largely a matter of professional opinion. This is a growing topic of interest to researchers, however, since young people's time on social media has steadily increased. According to a 2015 Pew Research survey, 92 percent of teens aged thirteen to seventeen reported being online every day, with 24 percent of them saying they were online "almost constantly."[51] In light of the American Academy of Pediatrics' recommendation that children and teens spend no more than one or two hours per day on entertainment media, such heavy social media usage is worrisome.

> "Kids view social media through the lens of their own lives."[50]
>
> —Jill Emanuele, a clinical psychologist with the Child Mind Institute.

Frequent social media use can take a heavy toll on young people's psychological well-being, according to a 2015 study from Ottawa Public Health in Ontario, Canada. Researchers studied health survey data from 753 middle and high school students. One-fourth of the teens used social media for more than two hours each day, and more than half were online for less than two hours. An analysis of their corresponding mental health data revealed that those with the heaviest social media use had the highest incidence of psychological disorders, such as anxiety and depression, as well as suicidal thoughts, compared with the teens who used social media less.

Although the Canadian study did not definitively prove that heavy social media causes mental health problems in adolescents, it strongly suggested an association. The issue is pressing enough to warrant further study, as the report authors write: "More research is needed to disentangle the relationship between the use of SNSs [social network sites] and mental health among children and adolescents."[52]

Other research has shown a different kind of problem among young people who are heavy social media users: the risk of becoming addicted. This is controversial, since not all psychology professionals believe that an activity (as opposed to drugs or alcohol) can be addictive. According to Bernard Luskin, president of the American Psychological Association's Society for Media Technology and Psychology, social media addiction is a real disorder that can be distinguished from habitual use. "We draw the line between habit and addiction when it interferes with living a normal life," says Luskin. He goes on to say that since social media definitely interferes with some people's lives, for them addiction is very real. "For some, social media is addictive and can be absolutely lethal," he says, "just like anything else can be—even water can be deadly and people do drown themselves. We need to be circumspect and never dismiss the problem and say no."[53]

It's All About Me!

As social media's popularity has continued to soar, some psychologists have become concerned about the associated increase in narcissistic personality disorder, or narcissism. Its name is derived from a Greek myth about a handsome young hunter called Narkissos (Narcissus). The legend holds that as Narkissos stared at his own beautiful reflection in a pool of water, he fell deeply in love with himself. In psychology and psychiatry, narcissism is defined as a greatly inflated sense of self-importance and an excessive focus on oneself and one's talents.

Narcissism is sometimes confused with high self-esteem, but they are not the same. According to Jean M. Twenge, a psychology professor at San Diego State University, people with high self-esteem value individual achievement, but they also value their re-

te a mental illness like depression to a particular activity,
t is using social media or something else.
2015 study showed that there was an association be-
e amount of time college students spent on Facebook
depressive symptoms they experienced. This correlation
e complex than it appeared, however. Students in the
o suffered from depression were not only active on Face-
t also often compared themselves with friends and fol-
their real-world social network. Therefore, researchers
d that it was the tendency to compare oneself with oth-

As they grow and develop, it is normal for young adults to experience some insecurity and lack of confidence as their bodies change. These feelings can be exacerbated when they peruse social media pages of teens projecting the image of a perfect, charmed life.

lationships and understand the importance of caring for others. "Narcissists are missing that piece about valuing, caring and their relationships," says Twenge, "so they tend to lack empathy, they have poor relationship skills."[54]

Twenge, along with noted narcissism expert W. Keith Campbell, conducted extensive research on the topic for a book called *The Narcissism Epidemic: Living in the Age of Entitlement*. Their research involved studying the prevalence of narcissistic traits among thirty-seven thousand young people who were born during three different time periods: the 1980s, the 1990s, and the 2000s. Twenge and Campbell found a definite correlation between the participants' birth years and their narcissism scores, which was based on the number of narcissistic traits they possessed. Scores were markedly higher among the youngest group compared with those born in the 1980s and 1990s, which indicated that narcissism is more much prevalent among today's youth than previous generations. "Over the last few decades, narcissism has risen as much as obesity," write Twenge and Campbell. "In other

The Facebook Experiment

The Denmark-based Happiness Research Institute studies well-being, happiness, and quality of life. To examine the role of social media in how people feel about their lives, the institute conducted an experimental study in 2015. The study involved 1,095 Danes who were regular social media users. They were divided into two groups: One continued to use Facebook as usual, and the other gave up social media for a week (the treatment group).

At the end of the week, the people in the treatment group were found to be happier and more satisfied with their lives than the Facebook group. Those who had given up social media reported having a higher appreciation for their lives and were much less likely to describe themselves as dissatisfied. Happiness Research Institute CEO Meik Wiking attributes the findings to social media users' tendency to compare themselves with others. "Facebook distorts our perception of reality and of what other people's lives really look like," he says. "We take in to account how we're doing in life through comparisons to everyone else, and since most people only post positive things on Facebook, that gives us a very biased perception of reality. If we are constantly exposed to great news, we risk evaluating our own lives as less good." Wiking urges people to remember that what they see on social media is not necessarily reality. "This constant flow of great news we see on Facebook only represents the top 10 per cent of things that happen to other people," he says. "It shouldn't be used as the background for evaluating our own lives."

Quoted in News.com.au, "Facebook Makes Us Feel 'Lonely and Angry': Study," November 11, 2015. www.news.com.au.

words, the narcissism epidemic is just as widespread as the obesity epidemic."[55]

Not so clear, however, is whether the high prevalence of youth narcissism can be attributed to social media. According to Twenge, though, there is a good possibility the two are connected. She adds that narcissists are known to have more friends on Facebook

and post more (especially provocat more active on Twitter. Although it i social media use causes narcissm sites are clearly influenced by thos higher than their fair share."[56]

Another psychologist is less sur teens are more narcissistic than Diller specializes in self-image and s whether insecure adolescents, like ations, are simply doing what teer are, by nature, self-preoccupied, an mental passage into adulthood," s young people's desire for attention, and to appear special and unique, adolescent development process. yes, it appears, entitled, superficial, a narcissism is not the same as typica Rather, says Diller, it develops as th factors, including one's family life, pe consider other factors—like parenta our celebrity culture and more—to contribute as well," she says. "While already existing tendencies, it takes flourish in a culture."[57]

Social Media and Depressi

Another phenomenon that has receiv known as Facebook depression. This Academy of Pediatrics as "depressio teens and teens spend a great deal o such as Facebook, and then begin to depression."[58] These symptoms can r spair to hopelessness and suicidal fe with many other organizations and ps lieves that depression related to social rious attention. Others disagree, argui

to attribu whether

One tween th and the was mo study wh book, bu lowers i conclude

The American Acade Pediatrics has identif a type of depression develops when teens and preteens spend a great deal of time on social media sites. T condition, known as Facebook depression is controversial, and its merit is debated b professionals.

ers—and invariably falling short—that led to depressive symptoms. Because Facebook provides unprecedented opportunities for such comparisons to be made, it would be logical (but not necessarily correct) for people to blame Facebook for depression.

According to lead study author Mai-Ly N. Steers, a social psychologist at the University of Houston, those who make such self-destructive comparisons will probably need to avoid social media in order to stop. "Facebook's intended purpose is for people to interact and feel more positively as a result," says Steers. "However, if you are experiencing the unintended consequence of feeling bad about yourself after using Facebook, maybe it's time to step away from the keyboard."[59]

> "There's a lot of social pressure to show that everything's great. It's a never-ending quest to be interesting and intellectual and unique, and strive to prove something to the world. You can't just be yourself."[60]
>
> —Rich DeNagel, who gave up Facebook because it made him feel sad, lonely, and depressed.

Research about social media and depression has also focused on the type of people who share prolifically about themselves. A few studies, for instance, have found that lonely people tend to disclose more personal information on social media than those who do not feel lonely. Other studies have revealed that when people who feel lonely get on social media, it makes them feel worse. This was true of Rich DeNagel, a former teacher from San Francisco, California. He initially liked Facebook because it put him in touch with friends with whom he might otherwise have lost touch. But at one point he disabled his account for several months, because looking at other people's pages made him feel sad and depressed. For the most part, DeNagel finds being on Facebook to be a lonely experience. "You don't often see people putting out that they're going through a hard time," he says. "There's a lot of social pressure to show that everything's great. It's a never-ending quest to be interesting and intellectual and unique, and strive to prove something to the world. You can't just be yourself."[60]

Beaten Down

As more people have become active on social media, online harassment and cyberbullying have become a formidable problem. Victims of this type of abuse can feel traumatized, demoralized, and totally defeated. Although this happens on all types of social media, some platforms make it especially easy, such as Yik Yak. Launched in 2013, Yik Yak is an anonymous Twitter-like bulletin board app. Although it was created especially for use on college campuses, and its developers say younger teens were never meant to use it, the app has soared in popularity among high school students. "One problem for the service is that it's being used where it's not supposed to be—namely, at high school," says technology writer John Patrick Pullen. He adds that anonymous social networks like Yik Yak can be especially risky for younger users "because they can be a hive of cyberbullying, racist barbs and hate speech."[61]

On Yik Yak, users make text posts (called yaks) that can be up- or down-voted by other users (yakkers). The higher the score, the more popular the post is with yakkers. Yaks can also turn into conversation threads with people commenting however they see fit. "Every post or comment on the network is anonymous," says Pullen. "Users don't even get a photo or avatar to distinguish themselves."[62]

A growing number of people are strongly against Yik Yak because its total anonymity invites bullying, threats, and harassment. One young woman who was a victim of this cruel treatment is Elizabeth Long. When she was seventeen years old, Long attempted suicide but survived. Afterward she wanted to do something to help other teens going through similar emotional problems, so she began talking to her peers about her painful experience. In response, some people at her school began bullying her with Yik Yak; one person said she needed to stop talking "about how she almost killed herself and go ahead and do it."[63] Other yaks were equally insensitive and abusive.

Even though teachers threatened anyone using the app with detention, the site's anonymity made it impossible for anyone to

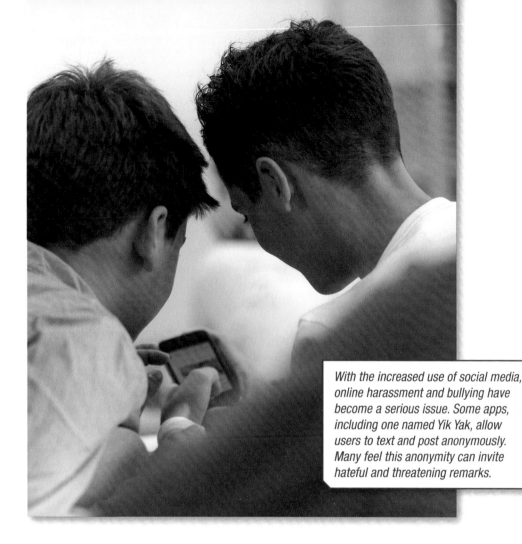

With the increased use of social media, online harassment and bullying have become a serious issue. Some apps, including one named Yik Yak, allow users to text and post anonymously. Many feel this anonymity can invite hateful and threatening remarks.

catch them, much less make them stop. "I was really sad when I first read the Yaks about me," says Long, "because after going through such a dark time, I felt like I was really doing something positive with my experience . . . but others just used it against me."[64] There was nothing Long, the school, or other students being bullied through Yik Yak could do about it, though, because users were posting anonymously.

Long refused to give up. Through the social change platform Change.org, she started a movement to petition the app's developers to either shut Yik Yak down or more closely monitor it. "The whole app is a set up for hate speech and bullying," Long wrote in a letter to the developers. "Teens have begun telling others to kill themselves and it is only a matter of time before this

Yelp for People

When searching for local businesses, people often use the popular social networking site Yelp. They can learn more about a business by reading reviews posted by those who have experience with it. In this spirit, in September 2015 a social media app called Peeple was introduced. Promptly dubbed Yelp for people, the app allowed users to evaluate people such as coworkers, ex-spouses, former friends, and/or neighbors as though they were commodities. Its introduction prompted outcries about the app being rife with opportunities for abuse and bullying.

Peeple's creators staunchly defended it, saying that people should be able to do the same kind of research about humans that they do about businesses. Opponents argued it was wrong to reduce humans to the level of commodities. *Washington Post* digital culture critic Caitlin Dewey writes:

> It's inherently invasive, even when complimentary. And it's objectifying and reductive in the manner of all online reviews. One does not have to stretch far to imagine the distress and anxiety that such a system would cause even a slightly self-conscious person; it's not merely the anxiety of being harassed or maligned on the platform—but of being watched and judged, at all times, by an objectifying gaze to which you did not consent.

In the face of widespread outrage and hundreds of negative comments, Peeple's creators took the app offline and redesigned it. In October 2015 they rereleased Peeple as a "positivity app," meaning one that solely focused on positive reviews.

Caitlin Dewey, "Everyone You Know Will Be Able to Rate You on the Terrifying 'Yelp for People'—Whether You Want Them to or Not," *Washington Post*, September 30, 2015. www.washingtonpost.com.

app actually ends a life."[65] As of December 2015 Long's petition had garnered more than eighty-four thousand signatures.

Bullying also occurs on other types of social media and can even spread into mediums beyond it. One such example is found in Lindsey Stone, a former caregiver for adults with learning disabilities who was brutally bullied online and in real life. As part of a prank gone horribly wrong, Stone took a disrespectful selfie at Arlington National Cemetery's Tomb of the Unknowns and posted it on her Facebook page. The photo was leaked to the public, and people became outraged. Someone created a "Fire Lindsey Stone" Facebook page on which thousands of people posted abusive remarks about Stone. News reporters wielding cameras showed up at her home in Plymouth, Massachusetts, and when she went to work, she was told to turn in her keys; she was fired.

For an entire year following the nightmarish ordeal, Stone barely left her house. "I didn't want to be seen by anyone," she says. "I didn't want people looking at me."[66] She suffered from insomnia and depression and was diagnosed with post-traumatic stress disorder. Because of her experience, Stone has become especially sensitive toward others who have suffered a similar fate on social media.

> "The whole [Yik Yak] app is a set up for hate speech and bullying. Teens have begun telling others to kill themselves and it is only a matter of time before this app actually ends a life."[65]
>
> —Elizabeth Long, a young woman who was bullied on Yik Yak after she attempted suicide.

Psyche at Risk

Whether social media can be hazardous to mental health is widely discussed and hotly debated. There are numerous reports of people feeling sad, lonely, or depressed after spending too much time online, as well as accounts of users becoming dependent on it. Cyberbullying and online harassment remain serious problems, with victims bearing emotional scars that may last a lifetime. These and other negative aspects of the online world highlight challenges that are likely to grow as social media becomes even more popular than it is today.

CHAPTER FOUR

Social Media, the Environment, and Society

On November 13, 2015, gunmen and suicide bombers launched a brutal, coordinated attack on the city of Paris. Almost simultaneously, terrorists struck an athletic stadium where a football match was under way, as well as a concert hall and several restaurants and bars. As the horrific events unfolded, people throughout the world learned about them in real time on social media. People in France used social media to tell loved ones they were safe; others reported about explosions and gunshots, describing the chaos as only those in the center of it could. "It was an instinctive human reaction to tell others about the violence," says BBC reporter Anne-Marie Tomchak. "Each word, image, and video posted to sites like Twitter, Facebook and Instagram tell their own story."[67] By the time the terror came to an end, 130 people were dead and at least 350 others had been injured. Then, again through social media, the world mourned along with France.

People Pulling Together

For decades, people have been able to learn about breaking news by listening to the radio and watching television. But social media has added a whole new dimension to news broadcasting; one of speed, immediacy, and realness. People hear live news faster than ever before—and unlike the past, anyone, anywhere can provide this news. During the Paris attacks, at the exact moment they were taking place, social media feeds were providing detailed information not only from news sources, but also bystanders who were in the midst of the bedlam. Social media, says psychologist Pamela B. Rutledge, allows people throughout the world "to instantaneously see and respond to the horror and to feel the sense of vulnerability and chaos. . . . Through the voices on social media, we see events and responses as they are happening with immediacy and authentic rawness."[68]

Social media also allows people to reach out to those who are affected by traumatic occurrences. "Not only do we experience what's happening to others," says Rutledge, "we have a chance to reciprocate emotionally, to show empathy and compassion."[69] While Paris was under siege by terrorists, and especially in the aftermath, social media gave people worldwide a platform to express their shock, sadness, and support for the French people. Facebook activated its Safety Check tool, which allows users to connect with friends and loved ones during natural or human-made disasters to verify that they or others are safe. Twitter morphed into a virtual message board with all kinds of information to help people get to safety. For instance, by tweeting with the accompanying hashtag #PorteOuverte (meaning "open door"), people in Paris offered shelter to those who needed it. The hashtag #RechercheParis ("search Paris") was attached to descriptions of loved ones and requests for information about them. The same hashtag was used to share happy news when individuals were found alive and safe.

Hashtags also helped social media users worldwide show their solidarity with the French people. According to Twitter spokesperson Christopher Abboud, the most popular hashtag of all was #PrayForParis, which accompanied 6.7 million posts in

> "Through the voices on social media, we see events and responses as they are happening with immediacy and authentic rawness."[68]
>
> —Pamela B. Rutledge, director of the Media Psychology Research Center at Fielding Graduate University in Santa Barbara, California.

French police stand outside the Bataclan concert hall in Paris, where a terrorist attack took place in late 2015. During the attack, social media feeds were receiving live reports from news services as well as bystanders who were in the midst of the bedlam.

a ten-hour period. Also trending worldwide after the attacks was #UneBougiePourParis ("a candle for Paris"), which accompanied photos of people burning candles to show support for the besieged city. All of these actions demonstrate the unprecedented way social media can connect and support people in times of crisis. "We can come together as a global community and express support and caring to victims of terrorism . . . with a magnitude far greater than was ever possible at any time in history," says Rutledge. "We also take strength and courage from this outpouring of collective positive energy and concern."[70]

Environmental Activism

The same collective strength that enables people to reach out and support others via social media has also been shown to bring about societal change. Environmental activism, for instance, has flourished in recent years largely because of social media campaigns. During 2015 Twitter in particular was abuzz with environmental "hashtivism," or hashtag activism. One example is the powerful, influential Shell No! (#ShellNo) movement, which communicated people's strong objections to Shell Global's drilling in the pristine Arctic Ocean.

A particularly important activity of the Shell No! movement took place in July 2015. A group of Greenpeace activists in Portland, Oregon, blocked a massive icebreaker called the MSV *Fennica* from leaving port to head back to the Arctic. Within two months Shell had announced that it was canceling its Arctic drilling program for the foreseeable future. After hearing the news, Kristina Flores, one of the activists, tweeted, "Feeling victorious! The Fennica turned around and headed back to the port. Another successful day of blockading! #shellno Arctic drilling!!"[71] Twitter erupted with jubilant messages about the victory with the hashtags #ShellNo and #SavetheArctic. Although Shell considered this a setback (and did not close the door on future Arctic drilling projects), environmental activism was shown to be a powerful opposing force—and activists have vowed to take similar measures to protect the Arctic in the future if necessary.

Another environmentally focused social media campaign was designed to call attention to the plight of endangered species. The 2014 #LastSelfie campaign was a partnership between the Denmark and Turkey World Wildlife Fund and Snapchat. The purpose was to make the public—particularly millenials, who are challenging to reach via traditional media—aware that time is running out for endangered species. Each ad in the campaign featured a selfie-style picture of either a tiger, polar bear, gorilla, panda, or orangutan, accompanied by narrative explaining the creatures' plight:

In a way Snapchat is a mirror of real life. The images you see are transient, fleeting, and gone too soon. They are unique, instant and yet only live for ten seconds. Our selfies are the same, not just because they are delivered over Snapchat, but because these are the selfies of endangered species. Their plight [is] heightened by the fact that before your eyes they simply disappear . . . as they will do in real life if we don't take action.[72]

After the narrative, the image stayed on the screen for six seconds and then faded away.

The #LastSelfie campaign was wildly successful, exceeding all expectations. In just one week tweets and retweets had reached 120 million Twitter users, meaning that at least half of all active Twitter users saw one or more of the ads. The World Wildlife Fund had set a month-long goal for donations to its endangered species fund and reached that target in only three days.

#BlackLivesMatter

Closely related to environmental activism is social justice activism, and social media has played a pivotal role in helping to further these causes. A powerful example is a civil rights movement known as Black Lives Matter, which was born on July 13, 2013. Alicia Garza, an African American writer and community activist from Oakland, California, was disheartened upon hearing the verdict in the trial of George Zimmerman. In February 2012 Zimmerman, a neighbor-

George Zimmerman (pictured) was found not guilty of murder for the shooting death of Trayvon Martin in 2012. Deeply disturbed by the verdict and racial hate she discovered online, a community activist named Alicia Garza was driven to speak out against the unfairness through Facebook posts that eventually inspired the Black Lives Matter movement.

hood watch volunteer in Sanford, Florida, had shot and killed an unarmed black youth named Trayvon Martin. A jury found Zimmerman not guilty of murder, which Garza says made her feel like she had been kicked in the stomach—and after reading Facebook posts about the verdict, she felt worse.

People were not only siding with Zimmerman; they were blaming Martin for what happened to him, as well as blaming black people in general. Garza was both sickened and angry, and she felt a deep need to do something to speak out against this unfairness. So on her Facebook page Garza posted what she calls a "love letter to black people." She wrote: "the sad part is, there's a section of America who is cheering and celebrating right now. and that makes me sick to my stomach. we gotta get it together y'all." A later post by Garza contained words that sparked a new chapter in civil rights activism: "I continued to be surprised at how little Black lives matter. And I will continue that. stop giving up on black life. . . . black people. I love you. I love us. Our lives matter."[73]

Garza's close friend, Patrisse Cullors, saw Garza's post and was inspired by it. She amended the last three words to create the hashtag #BlackLivesMatter, and the two women began promoting it. Another friend, writer and immigration rights organizer Opal Tometi, developed a social media platform on Facebook and Twitter where activists could connect with one other in support of the movement.

> "Because of social media we reach people in the smallest corners of America. We are plucking at a cord that has not been plucked forever."[74]
>
> —Patrisse Cullors, one of the founders of the Black Lives Matter civil rights movement.

It has taken time and has generated controversy, but Black Lives Matter has become a forceful movement, one whose goal is to end racism and inequality in the United States. "Because of social media we reach people in the smallest corners of America," says Cullors. "We are plucking at a cord that has not been plucked forever. There is a network and a hashtag to gather around. It is powerful to be in alignment with our own people."[74] Cullors, Garza, and other prominent black activists view social media as a virtual bullhorn for sharing their message with the public and inspiring people to join Black Lives Matter.

LGBT Pride

Another powerful social justice movement that is fueled by social media is that of the lesbian, gay, bisexual, and transgender (LGBT) community. This was especially obvious in June 2015, when the US Supreme Court made a historic ruling on a case called *Obergefell v. Hodges*. In a 5–4 decision, the justices ruled that the US Constitution guarantees a right to same-sex marriage and states can no longer ban it. When the decision was announced, social media went wild with celebration. Major corporations such as Microsoft, Motorola Mobility, Google, Uber, and Airbnb immediately posted celebratory tweets that were accompanied by the hashtags #LoveWins or #Pride. All over social media, posts and tweets were adorned by the iconic rainbow image, which is a symbol of the LGBT community.

Facebook celebrated the historic decision by allowing users to add a rainbow overlay to their profile photo, and Mark Zuckerberg led the way with his own picture. On Twitter, any tweets with the hashtag #LoveWins were automatically adorned with a rainbow heart, and the hashtag #Pride produced a rainbow flag. Other popular hashtags included #MarriageEquality and #SCOTUSdecision. On Google Search, any words that fell within the scope of the ruling (such as *gay*, *lesbian*, and *same-sex marriage*) prompted an animated rainbow banner of people holding hands. In Washington, DC, the White House lit up with a vibrant rainbow of lights, and official White House photographer Pete Souza shared a photo on Instagram with the caption, "Tonight. #lovewins."[75]

Collaborative Research

As the use of social media has increasingly become a way of life for people, it has helped foster the growth of a phenomenon called crowdsourcing. At its most basic, crowdsourcing is defined as the collective effort of a large group of people (the crowd) in order to accomplish some kind of work. This might entail the completion

The Best Side of Humanity

During the summer of 2010, a former bond trader and amateur photographer named Brandon Stanton moved to New York City with a very specific goal: to photograph ten thousand New Yorkers and plot their photos on a map. Stanton called his project Humans of New York (HONY) and also created a blog and pages on Facebook, Instagram, and Tumblr. Over a period of a few months, Stanton realized that his HONY project was taking a much different turn from what he had envisioned. Rather than merely plotting photos on a map, he was collecting real-life stories of fascinating people; as he published these on social media, the number of followers soared.

In 2014 the United Nations invited Stanton to do similar work in eleven countries, including Kenya, Iraq, and the Democratic Republic of the Congo. In 2015 he went to Jordan and Turkey, where he interviewed twelve Syrian refugee families who had been cleared for settlement in the United States. After sharing their photos and stories, in which he described all that the refugees had gone through during their escape to freedom, Stanton held a fund-raiser. In six days more than eighteen thousand people had raised enough money to provide each family with about $40,000. "That is a large amount for anyone," Stanton posted on the HONY Facebook page, "but when you are starting from zero, it is all the money in the world. These families lost everything in the war. Most have multiple children and significant medical needs, so our assistance will significantly ease the stress of starting over."

Brandon Stanton, "Humans of New York," Facebook, December 25, 2015. https://m.face book.com.

of major projects, conducting scientific research, or fund-raising for a worthy cause. The advantage of crowdsourcing is the ability to tap into the diverse creativity, intelligence, and expertise of hundreds or even thousands of people in an online setting. The project benefits in innumerable ways without being inhibited by geographic boundaries or other constraints. Data scientist and statistician Anna Gordon writes: "The emergence of crowdsourcing is due to the realisation that getting ideas from thousands of diverse minds is much more effective than leaving it to eight people [sitting] around a boardroom table."[76]

One type of crowdsourcing is crowd science, which is also called citizen science, volunteer science, or crowd-sourced science. In essence, crowd science involves people coming together (in a virtual sense) to conduct scientific research. "Imagine science based on massively collaborative efforts where tasks are divvied up,"[77] says Caren Cooper, assistant director of the North Carolina Museum of Natural Sciences Biodiversity Research Lab. As a good example of crowd science, Cooper cites Zooniverse, which is the largest and most popular crowd science platform and home to a wide array of projects. Zooniverse projects include helping researchers find fossils in Kenya, transcribing archival documents, categorizing photographs taken of Mars's surface, and scrolling through thousands of videos of chimpanzees to document their behavior. Tasks "can look like a hobby, a game, a puzzle, brainstorming, or even like mind-numbing drudgery," says Cooper. "Sometimes a project has to entice people in, and in other cases people are banging down the door." As varied as these projects can be, Cooper says they all have one thing in common. "The common denominator for all citizen science is collaborative research that includes members of the public in any one of a variety of ways."[78]

Other crowd science projects enlist volunteers to do tasks such as classifying animal photographs, examining cancer cell images, detecting solar storms heading toward Earth, or studying the Milky Way galaxy. Although some projects require technical knowledge from participants, most do not; volunteers only need to have an interest in science and be able to follow instructions. "The

Social Media Gets Political

In a May 2015 survey by the Pew Research Center, more Americans said they were using social media to connect with politicians than ever before. Specifically, the number of registered voters who follow political figures on social media doubled from 2010 to 2014. Reasons for this trend include people's desire to feel more personally connected to a politician or group, an interest in learning about politics-related news (hopefully before others do), and a belief that the information obtained is more reliable than information from traditional news organizations.

Political candidates have also increased their social media presence. Between July 2015 and February 2016, Republican presidential candidate Donald Trump's Twitter followers jumped from about 3 million to more than 6 million. During that same time period, Democratic presidential front-runner Hillary Clinton increased her Twitter followers from fewer than 4 million to about 5.5 million. Politicians' sense of social media's importance is reflected in the fact that most carefully screen their posts just as they would any public communication. According to *Economist* magazine, the posts of many political figures "tend to go through social-media management software and past the keen eyes of press officers" before being released.

Economist, "American Presidential Candidates and Social Media," February 29, 2016. www.economist.com.

key is to translate the complicated science into something that's easily done by people who don't need to understand the scientific details,"[79] says Henry Sauermann, an associate professor in the Scheller College of Business at the Georgia Institute of Technology. According to Sauermann, people have a variety of reasons for being involved in crowd science, including the desire to contribute to society or simply to pursue activities that interest them. One huge benefit of crowd science is that it provides opportunities to build understanding and support for science. "Many people don't have a tangible connection to science," says Sauermann. "Crowd science can give people the hands-on experience of science, and therefore a better appreciation of it." As public awareness of crowd science grows, Sauermann anticipates "an explosion" of projects. "I think we are really at the beginning of something big,"[80] he says.

The number and diversity of crowd science projects is truly staggering. An April 2016 feature story in *Scientific American* profiles more than two hundred past and current crowd science projects, one of which is called Zooniverse: Jungle Rhythms. Volunteers who are part of this project help researchers better understand plant life and vegetation in Africa's Congo tropical rain forest. For a project called Zooniverse: Shakespeare's World, participants transcribe documents handwritten by contemporaries of the renowned English poet, playwright, and actor William Shakespeare, which will help researchers better understand his life and times. Through involvement in the Humpback Tails Wanted project, volunteers help track movement of humpback whales between their summer feeding grounds in the North Atlantic Ocean and their winter breeding grounds in the Caribbean Sea. For the Canid Howl Project, participants help researchers understand the range of different vocal behaviors of canids (mammals in the dog family), primarily wolves, dogs, and coyotes.

Crowdfunding

In the same way that crowd science revolves around group collaboration, that concept also applies to crowdfunding; the latter, however, is devoted to online fund-raising, and social media plays a pivotal role in its success. Someone who wants to raise money for a particular venture (like a crowd science project or a new product launch) creates an online fund-raising campaign. This is done with a crowdfunding platform, a website designed to facilitate financial transactions and provides other services necessary for fund-raising. Once the campaign has been set up, social media is used to promote it to the public.

The largest and most popular of all crowdfunding platforms is Kickstarter. Focused on encouraging creativity and creative projects, Kickstarter was founded in April 2009 by three friends from New York City. Since then nearly 11 million people have backed one or more projects, more than 103,000 projects have been funded, and $2.3 billion has been pledged for those projects. One of the most successful Kickstarter endeavors in 2015 was Zombicide: Black Plague, which is described as the "ultimate zombie

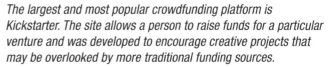

The largest and most popular crowdfunding platform is Kickstarter. The site allows a person to raise funds for a particular venture and was developed to encourage creative projects that may be overlooked by more traditional funding sources.

boardgame reinvented in a medieval fantasy setting! New survivors, new zombies, new equipment, and revamped rules!"[81] More than twenty-one thousand people contributed funds toward the creation and production of Zombicide: Black Plague, raising a total of $4.1 million. Other major Kickstarter projects have included the Pebble Technology smartwatch; the World's Best Travel Jacket, with fifteen features such as a neck pillow, an eye mask, gloves, a blanket, and numerous pockets for technology gadgets; a video game console called Ouya; and the Veronica Mars Movie Project.

Society's Gain

Social media has the ability to pull people together on a global scale, whether their purpose is to share information about a crisis, help save the environment and wildlife, support civil rights issues, conduct scientific research, or raise money for a fabulous new creative or business endeavor. The potential for social media in these realms is vast and will likely be limited only by human imagination.

CHAPTER FIVE

Social Media's Dark Side

Whether it is morbid curiosity, a strong sense of empathy, or a combination of both, people are often drawn to tragic events. Psychologists stress that such fascination is not abnormal; rather, it is simply human nature. "This is something across the board with humans in general," says clinical psychologist Matthew Goldfine. "Anyone who's driving on the highway and sees an accident slows down to rubberneck and find out what happened."[82]

Many have a similar reaction when they see graphic images or videos on social media. Although they may find the scenes cringe-worthy, something compels them to look anyway—and prevents them from looking away. This was the case on August 26, 2015, after a violent crime took place in Roanoke, Virginia. Because of social media, people throughout the world watched the gruesome details on video.

During a morning telecast, former WDBJ employee Vester Lee Flanagan shot and killed news reporter Alison Parker and photojournalist Adam Ward. Prior to pulling the trigger, Flanagan stalked his victims while holding a gun in one hand and his smartphone in the other. Once he began shooting, Flanagan recorded himself committing murder. Then, as people screamed and chaos erupted around him, he fled the scene. Shortly afterward he posted the chilling video on Facebook and Twitter, along with a string of posts in which he justified the murders. Within minutes Flanagan's Facebook and Twitter accounts were shut down—but it was already too late. Like a deadly virus spreading infection, the video had started to circulate throughout the Internet. "It's a darker use of social media," says Clint Van Zandt, a former profiler with the FBI. "There's something about us that lives vicariously through something like that. We want to see the violence, we want to feel the pain."[83]

Crime Comes to Social Media

The double murder in Virginia was one of the most horrific crimes ever shared on social media. Fortunately, such exploitation of the loss of innocent lives is rare—but crime in general is not rare on social media. In fact, it is common and its prevalence is growing. People are not always aware of this; because the word *social* has

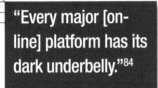

"Every major [on-line] platform has its dark underbelly."[84]

—Technology writer Fox Van Allen.

pleasant connotations, they do not necessarily associate social media with crime. But, says technology writer Fox Van Allen, "ever since people first started logging on to the Internet, there's always been a scammer out there looking to take advantage of people. Every major platform has its dark underbelly—there are e-mail scammers, eBay scammers and Craigslist scammers. Most recently, these scammers have turned their eyes toward sites like Twitter, Instagram and Facebook."[84]

Crimes related to social media nearly always involve what is known as social engineering. Sometimes colloquially referred to as "hacking of human beings," social engineering means using deception and manipulation to trick people into revealing sensitive or confidential information. "Social engineering is generally a hacker's clever manipulation of the natural human tendency to trust," says BullGuard Security Centre. Perpetrators who prey on trusting people use social engineering to obtain information that will get them unauthorized access to a system and the information that resides on it. BullGuard writes: "Social engineers rely on the fact that people are not aware of the value of the information they possess and are careless about protecting it."[85]

Since the early days of the Internet, online scammers have been looking for ways to take advantage of the system. Most recently, scammers have turned their focus on social media to gain access to valuable personal information.

According to the FBI, complaints involving social media crime have quadrupled since 2009. The bureau's 2014 Internet Crime Report, which was released in May 2015, shows that 12 percent of all complaints related to the Internet involve social media. In other words, out of 269,422 complaints in 2014, about 32,000 were social media related. Calling social media a "popular platform for criminals,"[86] the FBI says that as social media's growth and popularity have increased, there has been an associated spike in online criminal activity.

Click-Jacking, Pharming, and Doxing

Criminals who exploit people on social media often get creative in their pursuit of illegal activities. Although there are many types of online crime that involve social media, the 2015 FBI report lists three common examples, all of which involve fraud: click-jacking, pharming, and doxing.

Terrorist Tweeting Thwarted

Twitter officials have referred to their company as a global town square, a virtual meeting place where everyone is welcome. To Twitter's chagrin, however, this open and welcoming platform has attracted terrorists whose goal is to increase their ranks and spread their nefarious messages. In response, Twitter engages in ongoing efforts to identify the accounts of suspected terrorists and suspend them. In February 2016 the company announced that more than 125,000 Twitter accounts associated with violent extremism had been suspended. Company officials also announced that additional staff had been added to review reports of Twitter accounts connected to violent extremism, and to remove those accounts more quickly.

In a February 5, 2016, blog post, Twitter discussed these measures and emphasized its devotion to keeping the service free of terrorist activity. "We condemn the use of Twitter to promote terrorism and the Twitter Rules make it clear that this type of behavior, or any violent threat, is not permitted on our service. As the nature of the terrorist threat has changed, so has our ongoing work in this area."

The Official Twitter Blog, "Combating Violent Extremism," February 5, 2016. https://blog .twitter.com.

Click-jacking is a common Facebook scam in which unscrupulous advertising companies post links to fake news stories using sensational headlines. Van Allen shares some hypothetical examples: "Did you hear the tragic news? It seems that Lady Gaga has been found dead in her hotel room. Justin Bieber was stabbed by a crazed fan outside an L.A. nightclub. And don't even get me started about what Emma Watson did—I lost all respect for her when I saw this one video. Outrageous!"[87] Van Allen is quick to point out that none of these "news" items is real; rather, each is an example of click-jacking. If someone is fooled and clicks on a link, they will be redirected to a different link with malicious code. Facebook is then tricked into thinking the person "liked" the story or link, and it follows up by displaying the link to the person's friends. "If they click," says Van Allen, "they'll automatically like and share the scammy headline too. It's all a numbers game—the more clicks a scam site gets, the more it makes in advertising."[88]

To understand the fraudulent activity known as pharming, it helps to know about another type of online fraud called phishing. Cybercriminals pretend to be a legitimate company (such as a bank, department store, or the Internal Revenue Service) in order to deceive people into revealing their financial or personal information. Pharming is essentially the same thing, but executed via social media. "Scammers will present a link to a familiar website that many unwitting people will wind up liking and sharing—say, a link to a news story on *Time*," explains Van Allen. "If you click the link, however, you'll be taken to a spoofed version [of] the site where you'll be prompted for your login information for Facebook or some other site. Cyber crooks then take your credentials and use them to hijack your accounts."[89]

Of all the unscrupulous acts committed on social media, doxing is among the most vicious. It involves tracing someone, or gathering personal information about him or her, and then intentionally leaking that information online. This may include full names, addresses, phone numbers; any and all information that, as technology guru Mark Wilson explains, "could be embarrassing, personally revealing, or something that the victim would just rather keep to themselves." Wilson adds that although doxing is often carried out by hackers, that is not always the case. "Nearly all of us publish massive amounts of personal information online, and this can be very easily pieced together and used to gain access to even more data."[90]

Harassment

Cyberstalking and online harassment have been a part of online life for years, and the growth of social media has provided would-be harassers with yet another platform. An October 2014 report by the Pew Research Center found that 40 percent of Internet users have personally experienced some form of online harassment such as name-calling, embarrassment, physical threats, sexual harassment, and/or stalking. Of those who had been victims of harassment, social media websites (such as Facebook) and apps were cited as the most frequent platform for abuse. Half of those who had been harassed online did not know who had done it to them. And of all the people who had been harassed, it happened most frequently to young adults aged eighteen to twenty-nine.

Researchers are beginning to see that online harassment of women and girls is a serious and growing problem. Journalist and author Nancy Jo Sales discovered this while researching her book *American Girls: Social Media and the Secret Lives of Teenagers*. To

Researchers are beginning to see that the harassment of girls on social media is a serious and growing problem. To solve this will require a change in culture that is more supporting and respectful of women.

conduct this research, Sales spent two and a half years traveling throughout the United States. During her travels she interviewed more than two hundred teenagers to better understand how social media is affecting girls growing up today. To her dismay, Sales found that harassment of young females is rampant. She says:

> I would say what surprised me was the level of sexual harassment girls encountered online. The amount of "slut shaming" and sexual harassment that girls encountered on a daily basis was shocking. It affects their sense of what it is to be a girl in a negative way. To fix it, you really have to change the culture as a whole, the culture of social media, the cultural life in America. There needs to be more of a sense of having respect for women and girls.[91]

Digital Drug Dealing

It is no secret that drug users can find most any substance they want on the Internet. Today social media plays a big role in online drug sales, as an Albany, New York, news report explains: "The drug trade has a new frontier. It's right in front of our eyes and easily accessed by anyone. Whether it's Facebook, Instagram or Craigslist, dealers have an open market."[92]

In April 2015 a reporter from an Albany news station teamed up with Albany County Sheriff's Office investigator Bill Rice to see how easy it would be to buy drugs online—and it was far easier than either of them had guessed. "It's in plain view," says Rice. "It's blatant. Anywhere from marijuana on up to ecstasy, heroin; whatever you prefer, whatever you'd like."[93] Rice learned that there were hundreds of online drug sellers, and finding them was only a matter of plopping certain hashtags into a search engine.

"What surprised me was the level of sexual harassment girls encountered online. The amount of 'slut shaming' and sexual harassment that girls encountered on a daily basis was shocking."[91]

—Nancy Jo Sales, a journalist and author of *American Girls: Social Media and the Secret Lives of Teenagers.*

During the investigation, Rice was astonished at how bold and brash the online drug dealers were. One of them, with the obvious Twitter handle @518HeroinDelivr, sold heroin and promised prompt delivery to Albany. Another dealer clearly advertised his drugs on Instagram, including the prices he was charging for them, "telling us how much it is for Molly, which is ecstasy, MDMA," says Rice. "If you send him money, he'll send it to you either in an Amazon box or a FedEx box."[94]

James Burns is an investigator with the Drug Enforcement Administration who is in charge of operations in upstate New York. According to Burns, one of the main reasons online drug dealers sell on social media is because they are targeting teens. Since social media is so popular with teens, the dealers know it is the best way to reach them. "They are targeting our young folks because these are the folks that are the most technologically savvy and the folks that use these sites,"[95] says Burns.

Terrorists on Social Media

Among the most nefarious uses of social media are acts related to terrorism. International intelligence shows that terrorist groups such as ISIS use social media to recruit members, plot operations, and communicate with each other. Because they want the whole world to know about their crimes against humanity, terrorists also post videos on social media. Journalist Jason Burke writes: "ISIS videos include the executions of western aid workers and journalists, Syrian government soldiers, alleged spies and suspected homosexuals, a Jordanian pilot, Christian migrant workers, and others." Burke adds that the gruesome details of these executions are often on full display. "A representative sample can be viewed, entirely uncensored, with a few simple clicks on the device in your pocket or on which you may be reading this."[96]

On October 31, 2015, two weeks before the terrorist attacks in Paris, ISIS posted a video that encouraged young people in France to join its organization. ISIS had released a similar video on social media a month earlier that encouraged young French citizens to commit terrorist attacks. Other videos were posted on

Persin, the Pretend Predator

In August 2015 twenty-one-year-old YouTube celebrity Coby Persin uploaded a new video—one that sent a chilling message to parents and young people. The video demonstrated how easily an underage girl could be lured from her home by a potential predator. Persin was inspired to create the video after seeing a news story about a father whose twelve-year-old daughter was abducted by a twenty-seven-year-old man.

Persin created a fake Facebook page and pretended to be a fifteen-year-old boy. He then obtained permission from the parents of three teenage girls, explaining that he would friend the girls and then (under the parents' watchful eye) coax them into meeting him in person. The parents agreed, though they expressed confidence that their daughters would not meet up with someone they only knew from social media. They were wrong, however. Not only did all three girls agree to meet Persin, the oldest climbed into a van she was told belonged to his brother—where her parents were waiting for her with a stern reprimand. As for Persin, he was upset that young girls would be so naive, and especially that one would enter a van with someone she did not know. "At the end of the video I was almost going to cry. I felt sad for this girl," he says. "But she needed to learn a lesson and it can go way worse; this is nothing."

Quoted in Maria Coder, "Prankster Who Lured Underage Girls off Facebook Shows the Danger of Social Media: 'It Wasn't That Hard,'" *People*, August 12, 2015. www.people.com.

social media as well, and their purpose was also to recruit young people in France to join ISIS. "It would be simplistic to conclude that the terrorists of Paris committed the attack because they watched ISIS videos on the Internet," says Javier Lesaca, an associate professor at Universidad de Navarra in Pamplona, Spain. "But at the same time, there are significant grounds to suspect that the ISIS audiovisual communication through social networks might be linked with the terrorist attacks."[97]

Dangers for Youth

In terms of Internet-related crime, one of law enforcement's major priorities is crimes against children—and social media presents numerous risks for young people. The FBI writes: "Even with all the media attention on the dangers of social networking, we still receive hundreds of complaints per year about children who have been victims of criminal incidents on social networks."[98]

One social media platform that has law enforcement professionals especially concerned is Kik, an app that is used by an estimated 40 percent of American teenagers. Kik enables people to instant message each other and to share photos, videos, or other content. Experts warn that Kik can be dangerous because it enables users to identify themselves only by an invented username; thus, the app provides complete anonymity. "Kik is the problem app of the moment," says David Frattare, commander of the Ohio Internet Crimes Against Children Task Force, which includes hundreds of law enforcement agencies throughout the state. "We tell

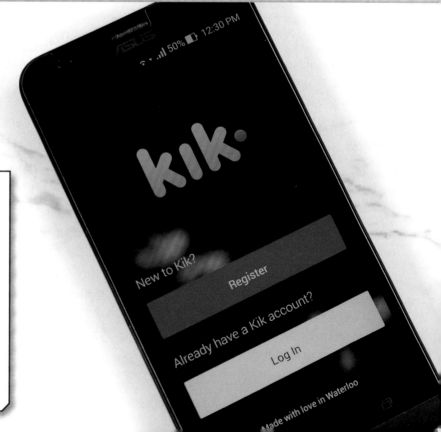

The social media platform Kik is used by 40 percent of American teenagers. The app allows users to remain anonymous as they share photos, videos, and other content. Law enforcement officers say that sexual predators use the site to hunt for unsuspecting victims.

parents about Kik, and to them it's some earth-shattering news, and then it turns out it's been on their kid's phone for months and months. And as a law enforcement agency, the information that we can get from Kik is extremely limited."[99]

In January 2016 thirteen-year-old Nicole Madison Lovell was the victim of a brutal crime that began with Kik—and the relationship she formed on the app led to her death. Lovell had become involved with David Eisenhauer, an eighteen-year-old student at Virginia Tech. Although she had not discussed her romantic interest with her mother, she showed Eisenhauer's picture and a thread of text messages between them to some friends who lived next door. She told them he was her boyfriend and his name was David, and she also said that she planned to sneak out that night to meet him.

> "The predators, the bad actors, will go where the kids are, go where the targets are. And these days they are online."[100]
>
> —Adam Lee, the special agent in charge of the FBI's Richmond, Virginia, office.

On January 27, 2016, Lovell pushed a dresser up against her bedroom door and then climbed out her window. Late that night her mother went to the girl's room to check on her, discovered that she was missing, and contacted police. A search party began looking for Lovell and found her body on the afternoon of January 30, 2016. She had been stabbed multiple times, and Eisenhauer was arrested and charged with her abduction and murder. "The predators, the bad actors, will go where the kids are, go where the targets are," says Adam Lee, the special agent in charge of the FBI's Richmond, Virginia, office. "And these days they are online."[100]

Unfortunate Reality

Social media offers people innumerable benefits, but there is also a dark and ugly side to social media—one in which unscrupulous individuals victimize innocent people, people are able to buy illegal drugs, and terrorists spread their messages of hate. Unfortunately, anyone who uses social media may be exposed to such ugliness, and the only real way to avoid it is to unplug and stay unplugged.

SOURCE NOTES

Introduction: A Global Community

1. Quoted in Alan J. Tabak, "Harvard Bonds on Facebook Website," *Harvard Crimson*, February 18, 2004. www.thecrimson.com.
2. Nico Lang, "Why Teens Are Leaving Facebook: It's 'Meaningless,'" *Washington Post*, February 21, 2015. www.washingtonpost.com.
3. Pew Research Center, "Social Media Fact Sheet," September 2014. www.pewinternet.org.
4. Amanda Lenhart, "Chapter 4: Social Media and Friendships," Pew Research Center, August 6, 2015. www.pewinternet.org.
5. Tommy Landry, "How Social Media Has Changed Us: The Good and Bad," *Social Media Today*, September 8, 2014. www.socialmediatoday.com.

Chapter One: Human Interaction and Relationships

6. Emily Rose Radecki, "I Met My Best Friend on Social Media," *Odyssey*, September 1, 2015. http://theodysseyonline.com.
7. Radecki, "I Met My Best Friend on Social Media."
8. Amanda Lenhart, "Teens, Technology and Friendships," Pew Research Center, August 6, 2015. www.pewinternet.org.
9. Lenhart, "Teens, Technology and Friendships."
10. Quoted in Julia Glum, "Online Safety for Teens: Are Internet Friends a Good Thing?," *International Business Times*, August 14, 2015. www.ibtimes.com.
11. Lenhart, "Teens, Technology and Friendships."
12. Larry Magid, "Magid: Teen Social Media Use Helps Maintain Friendships," *San Jose (CA) Mercury News*, August 6, 2015. www.mercurynews.com.
13. Quoted in Glum, "Online Safety for Teens."
14. Keith N. Hampton, "Is Technology Making People Less Sociable? No: Relationships Are Being Enhanced, Not Replaced," *Wall Street Journal*, May 10, 2015. www.wsj.com.
15. Hampton, "Is Technology Making People Less Sociable? No."
16. Alice Marwick, "Increased Social Support, Even Online, Is Beneficial," *New York Times*, March 5, 2015. www.nytimes.com.

17. Marwick, "Increased Social Support, Even Online, Is Beneficial."
18. Larry Rosen, "Is Technology Making People Less Sociable? Yes: Connecting Virtually Isn't like Real-World Bonding," *Wall Street Journal*, May 10, 2015. www.wsj.com.
19. Quoted in Chandra Johnson, "Face Time vs. Screen Time: The Technological Impact on Communication," *Salt Lake City Deseret News*, August 29, 2014. http://national.deseretnews.com.
20. Sherry Turkle, "Face-to-Face Friendships Involve Real Emotions," *New York Times*, March 6, 2015. www.nytimes.com.
21. Susan Tardanico, "Is Social Media Sabotaging Real Communication?," *Forbes*, April 30, 2012. www.forbes.com.
22. Tardanico, "Is Social Media Sabotaging Real Communication?"
23. Quoted in Johnson, "Face Time vs. Screen Time."
24. Tardanico, "Is Social Media Sabotaging Real Communication?"
25. Rosen, "Is Technology Making People Less Sociable? Yes."
26. Rosen, "Is Technology Making People Less Sociable? Yes."
27. Sherry Turkle, "Stop Googling. Let's Talk," *New York Times*, September 26, 2015. www.nytimes.com.

Chapter Two: Sharing and Oversharing

28. Kristina Doan Gruenberg, "When My Husband Died at Age 30, Facebook Became My Lifeline to the Outside World," *Washington Post*, November 30, 2015. www.washingtonpost.com.
29. Gruenberg, "When My Husband Died at Age 30, Facebook Became My Lifeline to the Outside World."
30. Quoted in Joshua Andrew, "How We Grieve on Social Media," *Atlantic*, April 25, 2014. www.theatlantic.com.
31. Quoted in Andrew, "How We Grieve on Social Media."
32. Quoted in *People*, "Social Reactions to the Death of Caleb Logan Bratayley," October 5, 2015. https://storify.com.
33. Quoted in Jane Ridley, "It's Good for Kids to Tweet Their Grief," *New York Post*, October 8, 2015. http://nypost.com.
34. Jennifer Golbeck, "Why We Overshare Online," *Your Online Secrets* (blog), *Psychology Today*, October 15, 2014. www.psychologytoday.com.
35. Quoted in Eleanor Black, "Too Much Information: The Perils of Oversharing Online," Stuff, November 8, 2015. www.stuff.co.nz.
36. Lenhart, "Teens, Technology and Friendships."
37. Quoted in Claes Bell, "How Oversharing on Social Media Can Cost You," Fox Business, August 21, 2014. www.foxbusiness.com.
38. Quoted in Kaplan Test Prep, "Kaplan Test Prep Survey: Percentage of College Admissions Officers Who Check Out Applicants' Social Media Profiles Hits New High; Triggers Include Special Talents, Competitive Sabotage," press release, January 13, 2016. http://press.kaptest.com.
39. Quoted in Natasha Singer, "They Loved Your G.P.A. Then They Saw Your Tweets," *New York Times*, November 9, 2013. www.nytimes.com.

40. Quoted in Alissa Reyes, "Social Media Can Impact Future Employment," *California Aggie*, February 14, 2014. https://theaggie .org/2014/02/14/social-media-can-impact-future-employment.

41. Quoted in Reyes, "Social Media Can Impact Future Employment."

42. Quoted in Stacy Rapacon, "How Using Social Media Can Get You Fired," CNBC, February 5, 2016. www.cnbc.com.

43. Quoted in WPIX, "Daycare Worker Fired After Posting About Hating Children on Facebook," April 30, 2015. http://pix11.com.

44. Sonitrol Pacific, "Going on Vacation? Don't Post About It . . . Until After You Return," September 1, 2015. www.sonitrolpacific.com.

45. Quoted in Todd Leopold, "The Price of Public Shaming in the Internet Age," CNN, April 16, 2015. www.cnn.com.

46. Quoted in Jon Ronson, "How One Stupid Tweet Blew Up Justine Sacco's Life," *New York Times Magazine*, February 12, 2015. www .nytimes.com.

47. Quoted in Ronson, "How One Stupid Tweet Blew Up Justine Sacco's Life."

48. Ronson, "How One Stupid Tweet Blew Up Justine Sacco's Life."

Chapter Three: Social Media and Mental Health

49. Quoted in Rae Jacobson, "Social Media and Self-Doubt," Child Mind Institute, October 12, 2015. http://childmind.org.

50. Quoted in Jacobson, "Social Media and Self-Doubt."

51. Amanda Lenhart, "Teens, Social Media & Technology: Overview 2015," Pew Research Center, April 9, 2015. www.pewinternet.org.

52. Hugues Sampasa-Kanyinga and Rosamund F. Lewis, "Frequent Use of Social Networking Sites Is Associated with Poor Psychological Functioning Among Children and Adolescents," *Cyberpsychology, Behavior, and Social Networking*, July 2015. www.cs.vu.nl.

53. Quoted in Emma Stein, "Is Social Media Dependence a Mental Health Issue?," *Fix* (blog), April 24, 2014. www.thefix.com.

54. Quoted in Lynne Malcolm, "Research Says Young People Today Are More Narcissistic than Ever," Australian Broadcasting Corporation RN, May 16, 2014. www.abc.net.au.

55. Jean M. Twenge and W. Keith Campbell, *The Narcissism Epidemic: Living in the Age of Entitlement*. New York: Atria, 2013, p. 31.

56. Jean M. Twenge, "Social Media Is a Narcissism Enabler," *New York Times*, September 24, 2013. www.nytimes.com.

57. Vivian Diller, "Social Media: A Narcissist's Virtual Playground," *HuffPost Healthy Living* (blog), May 21, 2015. www.huffingtonpost.com.

58. Gwenn Schurgin O'Keeffe, Kathleen Clarke-Pearson, and Council on Communications and Media, "Clinical Report—the Impact of Social Media on Children, Adolescents, and Families," *Pediatrics*, April 2011. http://pediatrics.aappublications.org.

59. Quoted in Jesse Singal, "Here's an Explanation for the Connection Between Facebook and Unhappiness," *New York*, April 8, 2015. http:// nymag.com.

60. Quoted in Quentin Fottrell, "Lonely People Share Too Much on Facebook," MarketWatch, May 21, 2014. www.marketwatch.com.
61. John Patrick Pullen, "You Asked: What Is Yik Yak?," *Time*, February 4, 2015. http://time.com.
62. Pullen, "You Asked."
63. Quoted in Helena Horton, "Yik Yak: Teen Bullied on the Anonymous App for Attempting Suicide Starts Petition for It to Be Banned," *Telegraph* (London), October 5, 2015. www.telegraph.co.uk.
64. Quoted in Horton, "Yik Yak."
65. Elizabeth Long, "Shut Down the App Yik Yak," Change.org, October 27, 2015. www.change.org.
66. Quoted in Ronson, "How One Stupid Tweet Blew Up Justine Sacco's Life."

Chapter Four: Social Media, the Environment, and Society

67. Anne-Marie Tomchak, "How the Paris Attacks Unfolded on Social Media," *Trending* (blog), BBC, November 17, 2015. www.bbc.com.
68. Pamela B. Rutledge, "Why Social Media Matters in the Paris Terrorist Attacks," *Positively Media* (blog), *Psychology Today*, November 17, 2015. www.psychologytoday.com.
69. Rutledge, "Why Social Media Matters in the Paris Terrorist Attacks."
70. Rutledge, "Why Social Media Matters in the Paris Terrorist Attacks."
71. Quoted in Jon Queally, "#ShellNo Showdown Results in U-turn as Rappellers Repel Arctic Drilling Ship," Common Dreams, July 30, 2015. www.commondreams.org.
72. World Wildlife Fund and Snapchat, "#LastSelfie," 2014. www.justfor this.com.
73. Quoted in Jelani Cobb, "The Matter of Black Lives," *New Yorker*, March 14, 2016. www.newyorker.com.
74. Quoted in Sara Sidner and Mallory Simon, "Break the Cycle of Violence and Silence," CNN, December 28, 2015. www.cnn.com.
75. Pete Souza's Twitter page, June 26, 2015. https://twitter.com/pete souza/status/614604095358283776.
76. Anna Gordon, "The Power of Crowd Science: Bigger and Better Ideas for Your Business," *Tech Radar*, February 16, 2015. www .techradar.com.
77. Caren Cooper, "Pearls Across the Zooniverse: When Crowdsourcing Becomes Citizen Science," *Scientific American*, February 28, 2013. http://blogs.scientificamerican.com.
78. Cooper, "Pearls Across the Zooniverse."
79. Quoted in PhysOrg, "Crowd Science Provides Major Boost for Certain Research Projects," January 5, 2015. http://phys.org.

80. Quoted in PhysOrg, "Crowd Science Provides Major Boost for Certain Research Projects."
81. Kickstarter, "Zombicide: Black Plague," February 25, 2016. www.kickstarter.com.

Chapter Five: Social Media's Dark Side

82. Quoted in Zahra Barnes, "The Answer to Why You're So Morbidly Curious About Tragic Events," *Women's Health*, August 12, 2015. www.womenshealthmag.com.
83. Quoted in Reid Nakamura and Itay Hod, "20 Deadliest Places for Journalists: TV News Shooting Death Exposes Ugly Side of Social Media," Wrap, August 28, 2015. www.thewrap.com.
84. Fox Van Allen, "How to Avoid the 3 Most Common Social Media Scams," Techlicious, May 26, 2015. www.techlicious.com.
85. BullGuard Security Centre, "What Is Social Engineering?," 2011. www.bullguard.com.
86. Federal Bureau of Investigation, "2014 Internet Crime Report," May 2015. www.fbi.gov.
87. Van Allen, "How to Avoid the 3 Most Common Social Media Scams."
88. Van Allen, "How to Avoid the 3 Most Common Social Media Scams."
89. Van Allen, "How to Avoid the 3 Most Common Social Media Scams."
90. Mark Wilson, "Doxing: What It Is, and How to Avoid It Happening to You [Infographic]," BetaNews, January 30, 2015. http://betanews.com.
91. Quoted in Brian Mastroianni, "Book Reveals 'Shocking' Sexual Harassment in Social Media Lives of Teens," CBS News, February 26, 2016. www.cbsnews.com.
92. Trishna Begam, "Special Report: Drugs on Demand," News10 ABC, April 20, 2015. http://news10.com.
93. Quoted in Begam, "Special Report."
94. Quoted in Begam, "Special Report."
95. Quoted in Begam, "Special Report."
96. Jason Burke, "How the Changing Media Is Changing Terrorism," *Guardian* (Manchester, UK), February 25, 2016. www.theguardian.com.
97. Javier Lesaca, "Fight Against ISIS Reveals Power of Social Media," *TechTank* (blog), Brookings Institution, November 19, 2015. www.brookings.edu.
98. Federal Bureau of Investigation, "Social Networking Sites." www.fbi.gov.
99. Quoted in Sheryl Gay Stolberg and Richard Pérez-Peña, "Wildly Popular App Kik Offers Teenagers, and Predators, Anonymity," *New York Times*, February 5, 2016. www.nytimes.com.
100. Quoted in Sarah Kleiner and Ali Rockett, "VCU Professor Says Nicole Lovell's Online Activities Should Serve as Warning to Parents, Teens," *Culpeper Star-Exponent* (Culpeper County, VA), February 14, 2016. www.dailyprogress.com.

Common Sense Media
650 Townsend, Suite 375
San Francisco, CA 94103
phone: (415) 863-0600 • fax: (415) 863-0601
e-mail: info@commonsensemedia.org
website: www.commonsensemedia.org

Common Sense Media is an organization that provides trust-worthy information on media and entertainment content to the public. A number of reports and articles about social media are available on its website.

Electronic Frontier Foundation (EFF)
454 Shotwell St.
San Francisco, CA 94110
phone: (415) 436-9333 • fax: (415) 436-9993
e-mail: information@eff.org • website: www.eff.org

The EFF is a civil liberties organization that advocates on behalf of the public interest with regard to Internet-related issues such as free speech, privacy, innovation, and consumer rights. The website's search engine produces numerous articles about matters related to social media.

Electronic Privacy Information Center (EPIC)
1718 Connecticut Ave. NW, Suite 200
Washington, DC 20009
phone: (202) 483-1140 • fax: (202) 483-1248
website: http://epic.org

EPIC is a public interest research center that seeks to focus public attention on civil liberties issues and to protect privacy, the First Amendment, and constitutional rights. Its website links to a number of reports and other publications related to social media.

Enough Is Enough
746 Walker Rd.
Great Falls, VA 22066
phone: (703) 759-6862 • fax: (703) 759-3810
website: www.enough.org

Enough Is Enough is a nonprofit organization that works to make the Internet safer for children and families. The website offers news releases, fact sheets, articles, and a link to the *Enough Is Enough* blog.

Family Online Safety Institute (FOSI)

624 Ninth St. NW, Suite 222
Washington, DC 20001
phone: (202) 572-6252
e-mail: fosi@fosi.org • website: http://fosi.org

The FOSI seeks to make the online world safer for kids and their families by development of public policy, technology, education, and special events. Its website's search engine produces dozens of articles related to social media.

Institute for Responsible Online and Cell-Phone Communication

PO Box 1131
200 Walt Whitman Ave.
Mount Laurel, NJ 08054-9998
phone: (877) 295-2005
website: www.iroc2.org

The Institute for Responsible Online and Cell-Phone Communication promotes the importance of digital safety, responsibility, and awareness. Its website offers information about "digital consciousness," as well as teaching tools, online safety tips, videos, and a link to the newsletter.

Internet Education Foundation (IEF)

1634 Eye St. NW, Suite 1100
Washington, DC 20006
phone: (202) 638-4370 • fax: (202) 637-0968
e-mail: staff@neded.org • website: www.neted.org

The IEF is dedicated to educating the public and policy makers about critical Internet-related issues. Its website offers information about the organization's current projects as well as news releases and articles about social media-related issues.

National Cyber Security Alliance (NCSA)

1010 Vermont Ave. NW, Suite 821
Washington, DC 20005
phone: (202) 756-2278
e-mail: info@staysafeonline.org • website: www.staysafeonline.org

The NCSA's mission is to empower and support people to use the Internet securely and safely in order to protect themselves and the cyber infrastructure. Numerous publications related to social media are available through the website's search engine.

Books

Danah Boyd, *It's Complicated: The Social Lives of Networked Teens*. New Haven, CT: Yale University Press, 2014.

Jon Ronson, *So You've Been Publicly Shamed*. New York: Riverhead, 2015.

Nancy Jo Sales, *American Girls: Social Media and the Secret Lives of Teenagers*. New York: Knopf, 2016.

Sherry Turkle, *Reclaiming Conversation: The Power of Talk in a Digital Age*. New York: Penguin, 2015.

Internet Sources

Moriah Balingit, "Millions of Teens Are Using a New App to Post Anonymous Thoughts, and Most Parents Have No Idea," *Washington Post*, December 8, 2015. www.washingtonpost .com/local/education/millions-of-teens-are-using-a-new-app -to-post-anonymous-thoughts-and-most-parents-have-no -idea/2015/12/08/1532a98c-9907-11e5-8917-653b65c809eb _story.html.

Nicolas Carr, "How Social Media Is Ruining Politics," *Politico*, September 2, 2015. www.politico.com/magazine/story /2015/09/2016-election-social-media-ruining-politics-213104.

Mike Elgan, "Social Media Addiction Is a Bigger Problem than You Think," *Computer World*, December 14, 2015. www.com puterworld.com/article/3014439/internet/social-media-addic tion-is-a-bigger-problem-than-you-think.html.

Julia Glum, "Online Safety for Teens: Are Internet Friends a Good Thing?," *International Business Times*, August 14, 2015. www .ibtimes.com/online-safety-teens-are-internet-friends-good- thing-2052238.

Happiness Research Institute, *The Facebook Experiment*, 2015. www.happinessresearchinstitute.com/publications/4579836749.

Marissa Miller, "The RIGHT Way to Handle Social Media Harassment and Bullying," *Teen Vogue*, April 10, 2015. www.teen vogue.com/story/how-to-handle-social-media-harassment.

New York Times, "Real Relationships in a Digital World?," March 5, 2015. www.nytimes.com/roomfordebate/2015/03/05/real-relationships-in-a -digital-world.

Julie Pennell, "How Social Media Can Actually Help Teens Suffering from Depression and Anxiety," *Teen Vogue*, August 6, 2015. www.teenvogue .com.

Jon Ronson, "How One Stupid Tweet Blew Up Justine Sacco's Life," *New York Times Magazine*, February 12, 2015. www.nytimes .com/2015/02/15/magazine/how-one-stupid-tweet-ruined-justine-sac cos-life.html?_r=0.

Websites

ConnectSafely (www.connectsafely.org). ConnectSafely is an interactive online-only resource for parents, teens, educators, and others who are interested in Internet safety.

Humans of New York (www.humansofnewyork.com). What started as a New York City photography mapping project has evolved into a global human interest site and social media presence, with tens of millions of followers.

Safe Teens (www.safeteens.com). This site provides information about staying safe online. It features articles about protecting privacy and links to other online safety resources for young people.

Sweety High (www.sweetyhigh.com). Designed especially for teenage girls, Sweety High is a safe social networking world. Visitors can upload videos, write, and create digital artwork, as well as interact with virtual friends. The site regularly hosts contests and online events.

INDEX

PICTURE CREDITS

Cover: iStockphoto.com

6: Depositphotos

10: Depositphotos

14: Thinkstock Images

17: Thinkstock Images

22: Depositphotos

25: Thinkstock Images

28: Thinkstock Images

35: Thinkstock Images

38: Depositphotos

41: Thinkstock Images

46: Apaydin Alain/Sipa USA/Newscom

48: Gary W. Green/Newscom

55: Shutterstock.com/GongTo

59: Thinkstock Images

62: Thinkstock Images

66: Shutterstock.com/nukeaf